1 MONTH OF
FREE
READING

at
www.ForgottenBooks.com

By purchasing this book you are eligible for one month membership to ForgottenBooks.com, giving you unlimited access to our entire collection of over 1,000,000 titles via our web site and mobile apps.

To claim your free month visit:

www.forgottenbooks.com/free793237

ISBN 978-0-483-77610-4

PIBN 10793237

THE GLORY OF GOD IS INTELLIGENCE

No. 2. DECEMBER, 1886. Vol. VIII.

THE CONTRIBUTOR

A MONTHLY MAGAZINE

REPRESENTS THE

YOUNG MENS AND YOUNG LADIES
MUTUAL IMPROVEMENT ASSOCIATIONS
OF THE LATTER DAY SAINTS

JUNIUS F. WELLS — EDITOR

PUBLISHED
BY
THE CONTRIBUTOR COMPANY.
SALT—LAKE—CITY

RUINS OF
NAUVOO TEMPLE

THE CONTRIBUTOR.

CONTENTS FOR DECEMBER, 1886.

THE CONTRIBUTOR.

VOLUME EIGHT. 1886-7..

THE CONTRIBUTOR COMPANY takes pleasure in announcing the commencement of a new volume of The Contributor with the NOVEMBER* number.

The progress of the Magazine, in developing home literature, promoting the growth of Mutual Improvement Associations, which it represents, and cultivating a superior taste for reading matter among the people, is well known. It stands in these respects at the head of all our local publications. It contains more original matter, in better shape for preservation than any magazine published in the interest of our people. Following are some of the leading features that will distinguish

VOLUME EIGHT.

The Rise and Fall of Nauvoo, By Elder B. H. Roberts, Leading Church History Series. Illustrated with fine, full page engravings—each a Souvenir of Nauvoo—embracing the following views: The Mansion, Nauvoo House, Old Parade Ground, Temple in Ruins, Joseph's Store House, Corner Stone of Nauvoo House (in which Original Manuscript of Book of Mormon was found), Residences of Brigham Young, Heber C. Kimball, Wilford Woodruff, Edward Hunter, Daniel H. Wells, and others, and PORTRAIT OF SIDNEY RIGDON.

Notable Indians of Mexico, By Apostle Moses Thatcher. An account of some of the leading men of Mexico, from personal observations, and including descriptions of Mexican scenes.

The Religions of Christendom, A series of articles explanatory of the faith and church observances of the principal religious denominations, by their leading ministers in Utah. The first of these, "The Episcopal Faith," by Rev. G. D. B. Miller, will appear in the November number.

Why I am a Mormon, By several of our best writers, explanatory of the faith of the Latter-day Saints, and experiences leading to its adoption by the writers.

The North Countries, A description of Scandinavian lands and people, including an account of the "Land of the Midnight Sun."

Biblical Cosmogony, By Thos. W. Brookbank. A scientific treatise upon the formation and development of the earth, harmonizing the Scriptural and natural evidences of the creation.

The Eastern Question. A series of eight papers upon this interesting topic which has for so many years been the subject of dispute and warfare between the Great Powers of Europe. The articles are from the talented pen of Elder J. M. Tanner, now in Constantinople, and his personal observations of countries and people, will add a peculiar interest to the series.

Christmas Story, A Prize of Twenty-five Dollars and THE CONTRIBUTOR SOUVENIR MEDAL will be given for the best Christmas Story. Short Stories will also appear periodically in the volume.

The Prize Christmas Poem, And the best poetical contributions of our local poets will adorn the volume.

Comments of the Day, Will take up the existing situation of the Latter-day Saints, religious, political and social, expressing the views thereon of some of our leading authorities. It will be contributed to by President Joseph F. Smith, Apostles Moses Thatcher, F. M. Lyman, John Henry Smith, and several others, "whose voices speak with no uncertain sound."

The Editorial and Association Intelligence Departments will be replete with instructive information relating to the Associations and the general interests of our young people. Officers of the Associations are requested to contribute freely to these departments.

We thank the public for past patronage, and ask its continuation for the future. Subscription: $2.00 a year, in advance. SUBSCRIBERS PAYING $2.25, IN ADVANCE, are entitled to have the volume BOUND at the end of the year, FREE, Send in your subscriptions without delay.

ADDRESS: ## THE CONTRIBUTOR CO.,.

40 Main Street, SALT LAKE CITY.

Remittances should be made by P. O. note, money order, registered letter or draft.

* In consequence of a disappointment in the type procured for the New Volume; we were compelled to order a new fount by telegraph. The delay thus caused, and other reasons which we think will promote the welfare of the magazine have determined us to begin the volume with the NOVEMBER Number, instead of the October Number as heretofore.

THE CONTRIBUTOR.

The Glory of God is Intelligence.

VOL. VIII.   DECEMBER, 1886.   No. 2.

THE RISE AND FALL OF NAUVOO.

II.

HAVING described the site of Nauvoo, and related the circumstances connected with its establishment as a gathering place of the Saints, it is necessary to return to the consideration of some events, which occurred at Quincy during the sojourn of the Saints at that place.

Paul, in his day, told the Hebrews that all were not Israel that were of Israel: so all were not Saints that flocked into Quincy with the Saints from Missouri; many of them were altogether unworthy of the association of the Saints, and preyed upon the hospitality of the people of Quincy to such an extent, that the Church authorized John Taylor, now President of the Church, to write the following letter; which was printed in the Quincy *Argus:*

In consequence of so great an influx of strangers, arriving in this place daily, owing to their late expulsion from the State of Missouri, there must of necessity be, and we wish to state to the citizens of Quincy, and the vicinity, through the medium of your columns, that there are many individuals among the numbers who have already arrived, as well as among those who are now on their way here, who never did belong to our Church, and others who once did, but who, for various reasons, have been expelled from our fellowship. Amongst these are some who have contracted habits, which are at variance with principles of moral rectitude (such as swearing, dram-drinking, etc.), which immoralities the Church of Latter-day Saints is liable to be charged with, owing to our amalgamation under our late existing circumstances. And as we as a people do not wish to lay under any such imputation, we would also state, that such individuals do not hold a name or a place amongst us; that we altogether dis-

countenance everything of the kind; that every person once belonging to our community, contracting or persisting in such immoral habits, have hitherto been expelled from our society; and that such as we may hereafter be informed of, we will hold no communion with, but will withdraw our fellowship from them.

We wish further to state, that we feel laid under peculiar obligations to the citizens of this place for the patriotic feelings which have been manifested, and for the hand of liberality and friendship which was extended to us, in our late difficulties; and should feel sorry to see that philanthropy and benevolence abused by wicked and designing people, who under pretense of poverty and distress, should try to work up the feelings of the charitable and humane, get into their debt without any prospect or intention of paying, and finally, perhaps, we as a people be charged with dishonesty.

We say that we altogether disapprove of such practices, and we warn the citizens of Quincy against such individuals who may pretend to belong to our community.

We have given this letter in extenso, because it bears upon its face the evidence of the honesty of the Church, and its disposition to treat the people of Illinois, who had so nobly and kindly received its members in the days of their distress, with candor. It also tells us of a class even then in the Church, who by the vileness of their lives gave some coloring to the charges subsequently so unjustly made against the whole Church. A class who brought upon the Church reproach—an unrighteous apostate element, which still lingered with the Church for the sake of advantage—the bane of the body religious.

About this time too, the good feeling entertained towards the Saints by the people of Quincy and vicinity was not a little endangered through the unwise course of Lyman Wight. He began the publication of a series of letters in the Quincy *Whig*, in which he laid the responsibility of the outrages perpetrated against the Saints in Missouri, upon the Democratic party, implicating not only the Democrats of Missouri, but indirectly the National Democratic Party. This gave much dissatisfaction to members of that party in the vicinity of Quincy, who had been very active in assisting the Saints; and a number of the leading men approached prominent brethren, who still remained in Quincy, and desired to know if the Church sustained the assertions of Lyman Wight. Elder R. B. Thompson wrote a letter to President joseph Smith on the subject, in which he protested against the course taken by Wight, because of the influence it was having on many of those who had so nobly befriended the Saints in the day of their distress. Besides it was altogether unjust, for no particular political party in Missouri was responsible for the black cruelty practiced towards the Saints. Those who were in the mobs which robbed them of their homes, burned their houses, ran off their stock, and who whipped, murdered, and finally drove the people from the State of Missouri, were made up of individuals of every shade of political faith, and of every religion, and many of no religion whatever. It was unfair then, under these circumstances, that the responsibility should be laid at the charge of any one party or sect of religion. So that Wight's course was not only doing much mischief, but was also unjust.

To counteract the evil effect of Lyman Wight's communications to the *Whig*, joseph Smith, Sidney Rigdon and Hyrum Smith, then the presiding quorum of the Church, published a letter in the *Whig*, from which we make the following extract:

We have not at any time thought there was any political party, as such, chargeable with the Missouri barbarities, neither any religious society, as such. They were committed by a mob, composed of all parties, regardless of difference of opinion, either political or religious.

The determined stand in this State, and by the people of Quincy in particular, made against the lawless outrages of the Missouri mobbers by all parties in politics and religion, have entitled them equally to our thanks and our profoundest regards, and such gentlemen, we hope they will always receive from us. * * * * We wish to say to the public, through your paper, that we disclaim any intention of making a political question of our difficulties with Missouri, believing that we are not justified in so doing.

Lyman Wight was a bold, independent spirited man; inclined to be self-willed and refractory. No one could control him; and even counsel or advice was usually disregarded—except it was from joseph Smith. A few years subsequent to the time of which we are now writing, Lyman Wight himself said: "joseph Smith is the only man who ever did control me, he is the only man who ever shall." But to joseph's words, Lyman Wight gave respectful attention, and bent his own strong will to comply with the wishes of the Prophet. He himself was a master spirit, and could apparently bring himself to acknowledge but one to whom he was willing to yield his own judgment, and his own will, and that one was Joseph Smith. And it is said by those acquainted with him, that in the Prophet's hands his spirit was as pliable as that of a child.

It was one of joseph's peculiar characteristics to be able to control men— men, too, who were themselves master spirits; who were themselves naturally leaders; and it is seldom, indeed, that such characters are willing to take a second place. But in the presence of Joseph Smith, they naturally accorded him the leadership. He was a leader even among master spirits. A leader of leaders. It may not be amiss here to inquire into the mysterious influence which the Prophet joseph exerted over the minds of others, by reason of which he controlled them, since this particular instance in which Lyman Wight figures, illustrates it.

In reply to the letter of R. B. Thompson, joseph admitted that the course of

Wight was unfair, and said the Church was not willing to make of their troubles a political question; but he also said that he considered it to be "the indefeasible right of every free man to hold his own opinion in politics and religion;" and therefore would have it understood that, as an individual, Lyman Wight had the right to entertain and express whatever opinion he pleased in regard to their troubles in Missouri; only intimating that care should be taken not to set forth individual views as the views of the Church. In writing to Lyman Wight on the subject, joseph did not upbraid him, nor peremptorily order him to discontinue the publication of his letters, or retract them, but he informed him that the matter had been considered in a council of the Church, and that the result was that his course was disapproved. But joseph took occasion to express his confidence in Wight's good intentions, and said:

"Knowing your integrity of principle, and steadfastness in the cause of Christ, I feel not to exercise even the privilege of counsel on the subject, save only to request that you will endeavor to bear in mind the importance of the subject, and how easy it might be to get a misunderstanding with the brethren concerning it; and though last, but not least, that whilst you continue to go upon your own credit, you will steer clear of making the Church appear as either supporting or opposing you in your politics, lest such a course may have a tendency to bring about persecution on the Church, where a little wisdom and caution may avoid it.

I do not know that there is any occasion for my thus cautioning you in this thing, but having done so, I hope it will be well taken, and that all things shall eventually be found to work together for the good of the Saints. * * * *

"With every possible feeling of love and friendship for an old fellow-prisoner and brother in the Lord, I remain, Sir, your sincere friend."

Throughout this whole affair it will be observed that joseph starts out with the idea that every individual is absolutely free and independent as to entertaining views and in giving expression to them, both in politics and religion, so long as he makes no one else responsible for them. That in correcting Lyman Wight he does it by appealing to the man's reason, and by pointing out the possible result of his course, which may be avoided. by a little discretion; while the whole communication breathes such a spirit of confidence in the man he is correcting, and love for him as an "old fellow-prisoner," that it was altogether irresistible. And this is the secret of Joseph's power to control his brethren. There was no petty tyranny in his government. He was above that. Every right he claimed for himself, he accorded to others. While his mildness in correcting errors and his unbounded love for his brethren knit them to him in bands stronger than steel. It was ever his method to teach correct principles and let men govern themselves.

Sidney Rigdon succeeded in escaping from the prison in Missouri before joseph and the other brethren, who were confined in Liberty jail. And on his arrival in Quincy, his position as one of the presidents of the Church, his education and eloquence, gave him the attention of the leading citizens of Quincy, and particularly enlisted the sympathy of Governor Carlin of Illinois. By coming in contact with him, and relating the cruelties practiced against the Saints in Missouri, he conceived the idea of impeaching the character of Missouri on an item in the Constitution, viz. "that the general government shall give to each State a republican form of government." And it was his point to prove that such a government did not exist in Missouri. His plan was to present the story of the Saints' wrongs to the governors of the respective States, before the assembly of the several legislatures, and induce as many of them as possible to bring the case before the legislatures in their messages. Another part of the plan was to have a man at each State capital armed with affidavits that would give the necessary information to the legislatures. After the action of the State legislatures the case was to be presented to Congress for its consideration and action.

To carry out his plans Geo. W. Robinson was appointed to take affidavits and collect general information bearing on the subject. And Sidney Rigdon secured a letter of introduction to the governors of several States and to the President of the United States from Governor Carlin, of Illinois, and Robert Lucas of Iowa. On the fifth of May, 1839, at a conference of the Church held near Quincy, Joseph Smith presiding, it was unanimously

Resolved: That this conference send a delegate to the city of Washington to lay our case before the General Government; and that President Rigdon be the delegate. And that Colonel Lyman Wight be appointed to receive the affidavits which are to be sent to the city of Washington.

Here the matter rested for a time, and the final execution of the scheme was intrusted to other and abler hands.

During the summer of 1839 the Saints who had been driven from Missouri continued to gather at Nauvoo and settle on the lands which had been purchased by the Church authorities. The violent persecution they had passed through in Missouri had well nigh wrecked the people. They had been stripped of their earthly possessions, until they were reduced to the most abject poverty. And the exposure and hardships endured made them an easy prey to the malaria that infected Nauvoo and vicinity. Another thing which doubtless contributed to make them unable to resist the ravages of disease, was the fact that a period of relaxation was following the intense excitement, under which they had lived for more than two years.

The spirit has such power over the body when it is once thoroughly aroused, that for a time it so braces up the body that it is almost impregnable to disease, and knows no fatigue. But this cannot continue long. It wears out the body; and as soon as the excitement is removed, then comes the period of relaxation when the body sinks down from sheer exhaustion.

Such was the condition of the exiled Saints who came flocking into Nauvoo, in the summer of 1839. They had reached a haven of rest. The fearful strain on the nervous system under which they had labored during the mobbings in Missouri and their flight from that State was removed; and they fell down in

Nauvoo exhausted, to be a prey to the deadly malaria. Such was their condition on the morning of the 22d of July. Joseph's house was crowded with the sick that he was trying to nurse back to health. In his door-yard were a number of people camped in tents, who had but newly arrived, but upon whom the fever had seized. Joseph himself was prostrate with sickness, and the general distress of the Saints weighed down his spirit with sadness. While still thinking of the trials of his people in the past, and the gloom that then overshadowed them, the purifying influence of God's Spirit rested upon him and he was immediately healed. He arose and began to administer to the sick in his house, all of whom immediately recovered. He then healed those encamped in his door-yard, and from thence went from house to house calling on the sick to arise from their beds of affliction, and they obeyed and were healed of their sickness.

In company with P. P. Pratt, Orson Pratt, John Taylor, Heber C. Kimball, and John E. Page, he crossed the river to Montrose and healed the sick there. One case is mentioned by all who have written on the subject as being very remarkable. This was the case of Elijah Fordham. He was nearly dead, and almost unconscious. Bending over him, Joseph asked the dying man if he knew him, and believed him to be a servant of God. In a whisper he replied that he did. Joseph then took him by the hand, and with an energy that would have awoke the dead, he commanded him in the Name of Jesus Christ to arise from his bed and walk. Brother Fordham leaped from his bed, removed the bandages and mustard plasters from his feet, dressed himself, ate a bowl of bread and milk, and accompanied Joseph to other houses on his mission of love.

All day the work continued; and to the Saints who witnessed the remarkable manifestation of God's power in behalf of the sick, the twenty-second day of July, 1839, is remembered with gratitude to Almighty God, who through the demonstration of His power that day, gave an indisputable witness to the world that He was with Joseph Smith, and had authorized him to speak in the Name of Jesus Christ. To the Saints, it was a testimony that God was with them.

We wish here to refer to a circumstance, connected with the period of which we write, that proves the devotion of the early elders of the Church, and under what hardships they were willing to carry out the purposes of their God.

A revelation had been given through the Prophet Joseph on the eighth of July, 1838, in which a commandment was given to fill up the quorum of the twelve apostles by ordaining John Taylor, John E. Page, Wilford Woodruff, and Willard Richards to take the places of those who had fallen through apostasy. The following spring "let them depart," said the revelation, "to go over the great waters, and there promulgate my Gospel, the fulness thereof, and bear record of My name. Let them take leave of My Saints in the city of Far West, on the twenty-sixth day of April next, on the building spot of my house." By the twenty-sixth of April, the day set for them to take leave of the Saints to start on their mission, nearly all the Saints had been driven from Far West, and in fact from Missouri; and the mob had boasted that that revelation of "Joe Smith's" should not be fulfilled. But after the expulsion of the body of the Church from the State, the Twelve at the risk of their lives returned to the temple site in the night, taking with them a number of Saints, transacted the business appointed unto them by the revelation; sang Adam-ondi-ahman, bade farewell to the Saints that were present, and started for England, though they were detained for some time in Nauvoo.

The latter part of the summer, however, found them making every exertion to continue their journey. Wilford Woodruff and John Taylor were the first of the quorum to leave Nauvoo for England. Elder Woodruff at this time was living at Montrose, and was rowed across the river in a canoe by Brigham Young. On landing, he lay down to rest on a side of sole leather, near the post office. While there President Joseph Smith came along and said: "Well, Brother Woodruff, you have started on your mission?"

"Yes, but I feel and look more like a subject for the dissecting room than a missionary," was the reply.

"What did you say that for?" asked Joseph, "Get up and go along, all will be well with you."

Shortly afterwards Elder Woodruff was joined by Elder Taylor, and together they started on their mission. On their way they passed Parley P. Pratt, stripped, bare headed and bare footed, hewing some logs for a house. He hailed the brethren as they passed and gave them a purse, though he had nothing to put in it. Elder Heber C. Kimball, who was but a short distance away, stripped as Elder Pratt was, came up and said: "As Brother Parley has given you a purse, I have a dollar I will give you to put in it." And mutually blessing each other, they separated to meet again in foreign lands.

On the twenty-ninth of August, Parley P. Pratt and his brother Orson started for England, leaving Nauvoo in their own carriage.

On the fourteenth of the following month Brigham Young left his home at Montrose and started for England. He had been prostrated for some time with sickness, and at the time of starting on his mission was so feeble that he had to be assisted to the ferry, only some thirty rods from his house. All his children were sick, and he left his wife with a babe but ten days old, and in the poorest of circumstances, for the mobs of Missouri had robbed him of all he had. After crossing the river to the Nauvoo side, Israel Barlow took him on a horse behind him and carried him to the house of Elder Heber C. Kimball, where his strength altogether failed him, and he had to remain there for several days, nursed by his wife, who, hearing that he was unable to get farther than Brother Kimball's, had a boy carry her in a wagon to him.

On the eighteenth of the month, however, Brigham, in company with Heber C. Kimball, made another start. A brother by the name of Charles Hubbard sent a boy with a team to take them a day's journey on their way. Elder Kimball left his wife shaking on the bed with ague, and all his children sick. With the assistance of some of the brethren they climbed into the wagon.

"It seemed to me," says Elder Kimball, "as though my very inmost parts would melt within me at the thought of leaving my family in such a condition, as it were, almost in the arms of death. I felt as though I could scarcely endure it."

"Hold up!" said he to the teamster. "Brother Brigham, this is pretty tough, but let us rise and give them a cheer."

Brigham with much difficulty rose to his feet, and joined Elder Kimball in swinging his hat and shouting, "Hurrah, hurrah, hurrah for Israel!"

And so continued on their journey without purse, without scrip, for England.

The departure of Elders George A. Smith, Reuben Hedlock, and Theodore Turley was but little less remarkable. They were feeble in health, in fact, down with the ague. Before they were out of sight of Nauvoo their wagon upset, and spilled them out down the bank of the river. Elders Smith and Turley were unable to get up, not because of any injuries they had received, but because of their illness. Elder Hedlock helped them into their wagon and they resumed their journey. They had not proceeded far when they met some gentlemen who stopped their team and said to the driver: "Mr., what graveyard have you been robbing?" The remark being elicited by the ghostly appearance of the Elders *en route* for England.

Thus in sickness and poverty, without purse and without scrip, leaving their families destitute of the comforts of life, with nothing but the assurances of the people, who were as poor as themselves, that their families should be provided for, they turned their faces towards Europe, to preach the Gospel to the highly civilized peoples of the world.

Shaking with the ague, and then burning up with the fever; now in the mansions of the wealthy, then in the hovels of the poor; now derided by the learned and self-styled refined, and now welcomed by the poor of this world who rejoiced in the message they bore—they journeyed on, never looking back, nor complaining of the hardships through which they were called to pass for the Master's sake. They had ringing in their ears the words of Jesus:

"He that loveth father or mother, houses or lands, wives or children more than he loveth me is not worthy of me."

And again they had the promise:

"There is no man that hath left houses, or parents, or brethren, or wife, or children for the Kingdom of God's sake, who shall not receive manifold more in this present time, and in the world to come life everlasting."

With this warning and this promise before them, they made their way by different routes, but at last met in England where an effectual door was opened for the preaching of the Gospel, and thousands with joy embraced the truth.

These men went out weeping, bearing precious seed, they returned bringing their sheaves with them, and had joy in their harvest. And what shall separate these men who endured so much for the Gospel's sake, from the love of God? "Shall tribulation, or distress, or persecution, or famine, or nakedness, or peril, or sword?" "Nay, in all these things they shall be more than conquerors through Him that loved them."

————

This number of the Magazine contains two engravings that will be of peculiar interest to our readers. They are Joseph Smith's Old Brick Store and the Nauvoo Mansion. The store is seen at the top of the page, the mansion below.

The store was finished and stocked with goods and opened for business on the first of January, 1842. Of this day Joseph says in a letter to Bishop Edward Hunter, who at that date was on business in West Nautmeal, Pennsylvania:

"The store has been filled to overflowing, and I have stood behind the counter all day, dealing out goods, as steady as any clerk you ever saw, to oblige those who were compelled to go without their usual Christmas and New Year's dinners, for the want of a little sugar, molasses, raisins, etc.; and to please myself also, for I love to wait upon the Saints, and be a servant to all, hoping that I may be exalted in the due time of the Lord."

But it is not as a store where Joseph acted as clerk for one day, that this old building is of interest, but because of other and far more important events associated with it.

The building, as will be seen, is two stories high; it also has a cellar or basement. The lower part of the building was occupied as the store; with a counting room, and a stair-hall leading to the cellar and upper floor ,partitioned off at the back. The upper floor was divided into two rooms. The one in the front was used to store away reserved goods; the one in the rear overlooks the grand old Mississippi and the opposite bluffs covered with timber, with here and there the rugged cliffs in view, which are seen at a few points along the river banks, in spite of the dense foliage of the trees growing on the bluffs. This view, with now and then a steamboat pushing its way through the placid waters of the majestic river, presented a splendid picture, of which the eye could never tire. It was also a retired spot, free from the bustle and confusion of the city and neighborhood, "and altogether," says Joseph, "is a place the Lord is pleased to bless." It was in this room that Joseph kept the sacred writings, and where he translated the greater part of the Book of Abraham. Here, too, Joseph first revealed to his trusted brethren the "Endowments," as now administered in the temples of God. In this room he taught them the glorious doctrine of the eternity of the marriage covenant and the plurality of wives. It was in this room that Joseph dictated to William Clayton, his private clerk, the previously received revelation on this subject as it now stands in the Doctrine and Convenants, at the request of Hyrum Smith, to have it committed to writing. It was in this room Joseph gave instructions in all things pertaining to the Kingdom of God; and revealed every key and power necessary for its establishment on the earth. It was here he seemed to roll off the responsibility that had rested upon him, to the shoulders of the Twelve Apostles; after which he rejoiced as a man who had finished his work, saying in effect, that if his enemies now should slay him, they could not stay the progress of the kingdom. Finally, it was here that the men whom God had chosen to be the leaders of His people often met and prayed for the redemption of Zion, and were instructed in relation to the final coming of God's Kingdom.

It will therefore be seen that with this unpretentious looking building, there are associations and events which give to it the sacredness of a Temple of God; and when all things that were enacted there shall be revealed, it will be held in remembrance as a sacred shrine.

The Nauvoo Mansion seen at the bottom of the page was the residence of the Prophet Joseph. It is an L shaped frame structure, the west front facing Main Street and the south front, Water Street. The chief point of interest in this building is that it was the residence of Joseph, and is the place where some of the happiest days of his life were spent. It was here that he entertained his friends, and some times his enemies, with that open hearted and open handed hospitality so characteristic of him. Here he feasted the poor, the halt, and the maimed among his people, as well as some of the first men in the State of Illinois. It was here that a few gleams of sunshine struggled through the black clouds that had over-hung his life and shed their light upon his path of life so filled with thorns. Finally at the close of his heroic career it was here that his mangled body lay in state, while his mourning people silently passed by, to look for the last time upon the form they loved so well. *B. H. Roberts.*

MARRIAGE IN ALASKA.—A diseased person among the Chilcats of Alaska is rather the exception, and prostitution as defined by them is punishable with death. At first thought their marriage laws seem very elastic, but such is not the case. Though they do not bind tightly they bind strongly, and the limits which are fixed are fixed indeed. The children always belong to their mother and are of her totem. This totemic relation is considered closer than that of blood. If the father's and mother's tribes be at war the children must take the maternal side, even if against their father. It is this law which makes illegal any marriage between members of the same tribe; though the contracting persons may be entire strangers, and unable to trace any blood relation. At the same time a man may marry his half-sister (one having a different mother) or a woman and her daughter—either at the same time or consecutively; for plural marriages are not uncommon, though they are by no means general. In very rare cases a woman has two husbands, oftener we find a man with two wives, even three; but more frequently met than either is the consecutive wife.

VARYING OPINIONS.

A lark was singing in a tree
　　Its songs of high thanksgiving
For light and love and liberty
　　And life among the living.
And as he flew into the sky
　　Sang sweetly to the linnet:
'Tis a happy, happy world, and high,
　　For God's kind love is in it.

A swallow sat beneath an eave
　　Her little ones caressing,
And gently to her mate did give
　　Warm love in tender kissing,
And as they watched the sunset's glow
　　In varying hues each minute,
Said 'tis a pretty world, I know,
　　With pretty birdies in it.

A mother rocking to and fro
　　A little infant tender,
Sings sweetly as the moments go:
　　"Kind angels, e'er defend her!"
And as wild kisses fall in show'rs,
　　From baby grief to win it,
Sings, 'tis a world of sweetest flow'rs
　　For darling babes are in it.

The babe with pretty smiles looked up,
　　Those smiles so full of sweetness,
That fill a mother's blessed cup
　　Brimming o'er with love's completeness,
And cooing soft, its blue eyes said
　　While kisses marked each minute,
'Tis a happy, happy, happy world,
　　With loving mamas in it.

A youth upon life's threshold stood
　　And brightly gazed upon it;
T' him its many paths seemed good
　　His eager soul rushed on it!

Love, science, glory, beckon bright,
　　And eager to begin it,
Cries, 'tis a world of glorious light,
　　For heavenly truth is in it!

A maiden sat beneath a tree,
　　And sadly looking skyward,
Bewailed her loss of purity,
　　And cursed a lover wayward;
And as she gazed into her heart
　　So full of dark despairing,
Said, 'tis a wicked, weary world,
　　With oceans of deep care in.

An aged pair beyond life's noon
　　And bowed by earth's disaster,
To whom could never come to soon
　　The summons of the Master;
While counting o'er their toils and grief
　　Dead hopes and tribulations,
Declared it truly their belief,
　　'Twas a world of sore vexations.

Old Time's voice mingled with the rest
　　As well he plied his sickle;
Earth's glories yield at his behest,
　　False pride and fortunes fickle.
And moving fast he cried in glee;
　　Life's thread—I soon can spin it!
Oh, 'tis a fine old world for me,
　　Mold, dust, decay are in it!

The angel reading o'er the notes
　　Which he had written truly,
Though striving still to hide the blots
　　Which Mercy mourned for duly;
Said, as the scroll he wide unfurled
　　And deeply gazed within it,
'Tis a happy, weary, wicked world
　　With crazy people in it!

Ruby Lamont

BERMUDA.

BERMUDA sits alone in the ocean, seven hundred stormy miles from New York, and six hundred and twenty-five from Charleston, in the same parallel of latitude. The ships of the Quebec Steamship Company sail once in two weeks from the metropolis, bearing Bermudaward hundreds of tired men and women, who have heard glowing reports of the nerve-bracing powers of the beautiful Summer Islands, and long for the peace and serenity · of which ocean travelers tell. The Atlantic is dark and billowy; the Gulf Stream tempestuous as the English Channel from Dover to Calais; but the passenger who climbs wearily to the swaying deck when the lighthouse on Gibb's Hill looms into view, beholds· a wide expanse of azure water, deep, delicious and at rest, encircling with all its varying tints the low islands of his dreams.

It was not long ago that few people left the common water ways of journeying to visit these small neighbors of ours; but now large hotels overlook the great sound, and the American is a familiar figure in the streets of Hamilton the White. The deep, rich color of the Bermudian sea begins just where the leaden-black disappears. The Islands seem brown as the Autumn leaves of New England at first, but when the negro pilot can be seen putting out to sea, to guide the steamer safely among the treacherous reefs, the green hue of the cedar-trees appears, and soon the snow-white houses of coral-stone glisten among them like huge blocks of Italian marble. Tradition says that there are three hundred and sixty-five islands in the group—one for every day of the year. Possibly there are a thousand, if every tiny rock that lifts its head above water at low tide is counted. They lie in the shape of a shepherd's crook, stretching from northwest to southwest, in latitude thirty-two degrees twenty minutes north and longitude sixty-four degrees and forty-one minutes west; and the area of all is just nineteen square miles.

The New York steamer, coming from the northeast, sails around the Island of St. George's, past the quaint white town which was old when our New England colonies were young, and enters the great sound where the dockyard of Ireland Island is alive with ships in stocks and busy workmen everywhere. The blue Bermudian sea is still as mirrored water there; and the only sounds to be heard, breaking strangely on the stillness, come from the hammers of the carpenters and the engine of the small steamer Moondyne, puffing its way from Hamilton to get the semi-weekly mail. If the tide is right, we can sail at once to the "Continent" and the City of Hamilton, taking a tortuous course among the small islands, dodging the coral reefs and sunken rocks, past the powder magazine, where guards walk slowly to and fro all day, along the shore of Fairy Land, and at last into the Harbor of Hamilton. The dock is alive with negroes and donkeys, both of the drollest sort. "How's onions?" calls some one from the shore; and a spirit of rare delight fills all the place when the monosyllabic but sufficient answer comes from a lusty throat, "Up!" "Onions is up" means a great deal to the tiller of Bermuda's shallow soil; shallow to be sure, but wonderfully productive year after year.

Though there may be three hundred and sixty-five or more islands in this singular group, only six are inhabited. The largest are the Mainland, St. David's, St. George's, Somerset and Ireland. Upon Boaz Island, lying between the two latter, are the great prisons where English convicts were once confined, now transformed into barracks for the royal troops, There are only two villages in the islands, though scarcely a foot of the tillable land is uncultivated. St. George's is the oldest; and this suggests the interesting history of the Summer Islands.

It was in 1515 that Juan Bermudez sailed from Cuba for Spain with a cargo of hogs. His ship, the *Garza*, wandered somewhat from her course, and finally the islands rose into view, above what the Spaniards had looked upon as an empty ocean. Bermudez judged that the islands were uninhabited, and he sent a few hogs ashore, to breed and multiply. Just as he was preparing to land himself, a gale from the north blew up, and he was forced to set sail without once placing foot upon the land of his discovery. He had with him, however, Gonzalez Oviedo, the historical writer, who has left us a quaint account of the voyage and islands as seen from the *Garza*. Spaniards did not try to settle there, though the King of Spain granted the islands to Ferdinand Camelo, a Portuguese. Camelo sailed for the Bermudas in 1543; he landed on the south shore, and carved in the rock his initials and the date of his appearance. The letters can still be seen, say the natives, though I never could discover them. People in the old world, who had heard vague reports of the small islands far away, held them in superstitious awe as the abode of devils and monsters, a place of enchantment where ghosts dwelt in darksome caves, and the lives of men were not safe.

Fifty-eight years afterward, Henry May, an English buccaneer, who happened to be on board a French ship, was wrecked upon the Bermuda coast. A few seamen and the officers got ashore, and after working for five months, constructed a rude ship, in which they sailed away. They found the islands covered with a heavy growth of cedar trees. A great drove of enormous hogs, descendants, doubtless, of the ones which Bermudez sent ashore, were running wild all about. Spiders crept over the rocks and the shaggy trunks of the green trees. May's story of the wonderful beauty of the Bermudas stirred the spirit of adventure among the English, and, in 1609, when Virginia was beginning to be colonized, Sir Thomas Gates and Sir George Somers sailed on a voyage of discovery with a fleet of nine ships. A great storm came up, the ships were widely scattered, and the vessel of the leaders, fittingly named the *Sea Adventure*, sprung aleak, and after a time was run ashore upon the Bermuda coast. The entire crew escaped. Turtles and shell-fish furnished food for the castaways, and they set about building ships. Many of the crew did not want to leave the island to which disaster had brought them. After the weary weeks upon the turbulent ocean, the islands seemed like Eden to them; and they were willing to live and die in that land of perpetual Summer. However, Sir George and Sir Thomas wanted to get to the colony in Virginia, and they blocked successfully the plans of several conspirators. On the tenth of May the boats were finished, and with a fair wind they sailed for the New World. They reached Jamestown after a pleasant voyage of thirteen days, and found the colonists there in terrible straits. Supplies were gone, and famine was upon them.

Sir George, who was a man of rare nobility, started back to Bermuda to found a settlement from whence supplies might be sent to the stricken colonists; but old age was upon him, his exertions had worn him out, and he had scarcely reached the islands when he died. His companions were terror-stricken, and, imagining the islands accursed, sailed away for England with the embalmed body of their leader. His heart, however, was buried in the little village which bears his name; and on a marble tablet there may be read this inscription: "Near this spot was interred, in the year 1610, the heart of the heroic Admiral Sir George Somers, Kt., who nobly sacrificed his life to carry succor to the infant and suffering plantation, now the State of Virginia. To preserve his name to future ages near the scene of his memorable shipwreck of 1609, the Governor and Commander-in-Chief of this colony, for the time being, caused this tablet to be erected. 1876." This memorial was raised by the good Governor Lefroy, whose name Bermudians always mention with affection and respect.

The travelers who returned to England told marvelous stories about the fertility of Bermudian lands. In 1610 a colonization company was formed in London, and sixty emigrants, in charge of Richard Moore, who was appointed governor of the islands, were sent out to the new land. Moore founded and named the town of St. George's; and for many years afterward the Bermudas were known upon maps as the Somers Islands. For two hundred years St. George's was the capital of the country. Governor Moore built forts for the protection of the harbor, and he had need of them; for pirates were common, and their ships often tried to enter the port. Emigrants came in numbers of two or three hundred a year, when matters were fairly settled, and they quarreled constantly among themselves. Moore was not much of a governor, say the records, and after a time the English Government sent out Daniel Tucker, who was something of a tyrant, but full of energy. The cedars being the only native trees, Governor Tucker sent to the West Indies for pawpaws, pineapples, bananas, palms, sugar-cane and oranges; and also introduced slavery, by procuring two bondmen, an Indian and a negro. Tucker abused the settlers and treated them very much as slaves, and some of them ventured to sea in leaky ships, preferring the chance of drowning to such an existence as the stern commander led them. About the year 1620 Tucker was recalled, and Governor Butler sent over in his stead; and this gentleman summoued a General Assembly, consisting of bailiffs, burgesses, clerks and secretaries. He also built forts, and undertook to connect the islands by bridges.

During the years that followed, the Bermudians multiplied and suffered much, as did the colonists in America. They had good governors and bad, and when the Revolutionary War began, the sympathies of the islanders were largely with the rebels in the colonies. General Washington wrote them a letter, and a large amount of powder was obtained from them, with which the American troops were able to make the British evacuate Boston.

At the close of the eighteenth century the Bermudians were prosperous and happy, the islands were blooming with fruits and flowers, and it seemed that the time of misery and starvation was ended. Since that time the Bermudians have multiplied largely in numbers; and their relations with our Government have always been cordial, save when the Civil War was raging, and the islands were the rendezvous of blockade-runners. As time passed, hundreds of slaves were bought by the islanders, and they were kept in servitude until the liberation of all bondmen in the British Colonies took place. The war of the Revolution proved the importance of Bermuda as a naval station, and in 1810 the British began to build a dockyard on Ireland Island, and erect forts along the coast. It turned out to be a slow and expensive business; and in 1842 convicts were sent over to be used upon the works. Three hundred came in the first ship, and within six years there were one thousand five hundred of them there. As time passed the beautiful islands became an awful penal colony—the home of more than nine thousand convicts. Many of them died with yellow fever in the dark hulks of stranded ships, where they were kept, and after a time their importation ceased, to the delight of the native-born Bermudians, who felt that their presence was like a fearful pestilence in the Isles of Summer.

Bermuda is the top of a submarine mountain about three miles high. The coral insects built up with their minute bodies to the very surface of the sea, and then the waves did the rest of it—washing into the central "pond" fragments of shells and corals, and forming, as ages passed, the peaks upon which the Bermudians have their homes. If the ocean could be emptied, the white houses of the island would rest high and dry upon a tremendous mountain three miles from the bottom lands below. Fifteen miles to the north of the islands rises to-day a solitary rock, all that is left of a sunken Bermuda, over which the cedar trees waved their branches no one knows how many centuries ago.

When the Bermudian wants to build a

house, he scrapes away the earth, digs out the coral stone beneath, and uses it for bricks. This coral rock is soft when first exposed to the air, but as time passes it grows hard as marble; and the oldest house is always the strongest. The excavation made by removing the stone, leaves a capital cellar. Building material is cheap, when it can be had for the digging, and so it happens that all Bermudians can dwell in marble halls. The stone house is the rule, the wooden dwelling a curiosity, in Bermuda.

There are no minerals on the islands, no stream of fresh water, no fresh water ponds. "What do you drink, and how do you live, then?" asks the stranger. "Very comfortably," says the native. According to a Government regulation every house must have its water tank; and it rains so often in the islands that there is an almost constant trickling from the clean stone roofs into the cool, delicious reservoirs below. The soil is always moist enough, and seems never to "run out," as would naturally be expected in so old a country. Almost everything grows upon it, except our apple trees, and the gardener tries faithfully to raise this northern fruit beside the waving palm and the banana stalk hung with its golden fruit.

I landed in Bermuda one day in March. The voyage had been rough, and the mercury was far below zero when I left New York. What a contrast, then, to wake up in Summer sunshine, to feel the warm breezes blowing from the sea, to behold streets lined with flowering oleanders, and hear the songs of birds upon the Pride of India trees. It was Hamilton, the capital city, a place of two thousand people. The traveler who has just left our bustling cities, is struck with the fact that no one seems in a hurry. At ten in the morning, scarcely half of the stores on Front Street, facing the bay, are open; and often at noonday the doors of the business houses are locked, while the proprietor goes away to take a rest. It is said that one merchant there has not had a consignment of goods since 1858, and still thinks that business is capital. It does not cost

much to live in Bermuda, unless you happen to be a tourist.

Hamilton itself is interesting, but the country places are far more attractive. The drives are beautiful, the landscape superb, every one courteous, and the air very tonic, which sends the blood thrilling through the veins. "You must see the north shore," says a friend who came to Bermuda before me, "and then you must go to St. George's, and everywhere else!" This was indeed a programme with a vengeance; but when I thought that nineteen square miles might easily be covered in eight weeks, I took courage. However, there is probably no inhabited place of the same area in the world where there are so many things of interest. The wonders of the sea, the beauties of the land and sky, are on every hand, and no lover of nature in her most beautiful shapes and phases can suffer ennui there.

It was only a short walk to the north shore, where a stiff wind was blowing, which rustled the leaves of the palms, and sent the small ground doves, which were creeping about and cooing softly, to the shelter of the rocks and banks. Far out to sea the white caps were visible, and beyond them, on the horizon line, a tint of rose, delicate and illusive. Nearer was the deep blue of the ocean above the reefs; and in the quiet bays, at the foot of the cliffs, an emerald green possessed the water, and the ripples that burst in wavelets against the rocks, threw into the air millions of jewels more beautiful than those encircled by bands of gold. Far away to the right lay St. George's, dimly visible, and to the left loomed up the fortifications of Ireland Island, opposite rugged Spanish Point. Now and then white sails flew past in the distance, and one great ship came into view. The road from Hamilton to the North Shore is picturesque and beautiful. To make it level, passages have been cut through the hills, and often the walls thus made on either side are twenty, thirty or forty feet high. Flowering shrubs and the curious air plant grow in the crevices, and the effect is unique and rarely beautiful.

Bermuda is divided into parishes—"tribes" they used to be called in the old days—and it is only a stone's throw from Hamilton to Paget. A negro ferryman, with a calabash cup for his contribution-box, rows slowly back and forth across the harbor all day long, and the landing-place is at a beautiful spot beneath the trees. The walk to the south shore from there is shady and cool, leading past Paget church, and through a lane to the blue ocean. On the south shore is a smooth, hard beach, over which sea-bubbles, like marbles of amber, are rolled by the prevailing wind. At each end of the beach are huge cliffs, and here and there tremendous rocks that are slowly wasting away before the waves.

Tradition says that Shakspeare, having read Sir George Somers' account of the Bermudas, made the islands the scene of "The Tempest," and that *Prospero's* very cave was situated on the south shore where *Caliban* climbed over the rocks, and witches cast their spells. The belief that Bermuda is the actual scene of "The Tempest" is founded largely on the reference in these lines, where the spirit tells his master that

"Safely in harbor
Is the king's ship; in the deep nook, where once
Thou call'st me up at midnight to fetch dew
From the still-vexed Bermoothes, there she's hid!"

Sang *Ariel:*

"Come unto these yellow sands,
Full fathom five thy father lies;
  Of his bones are coral made:
Those are pearls that were his eyes,
  Nothing of him that doth fade,
But doth suffer a sea-change
Into something rich and strange."

One of the loveliest excursions in Bermuda is from Hamilton to Tucker Town, and from there through Castle Harbor to St. George's. With a single square-sail set, we started in a whaleboat one bright April day from the little dock in Tucker Town, bound first for Castle Island. We beat about for a long time, and finally landed on the point of the mainland. We found rude steps cut in the rock, and clambered up to the smooth plain above, were grasses were growing,

and innumerable seagulls flying over head. Under this point is a cave, known as the "Queen's White Hall," on a level with the sea. We entered this at low tide, and found therein a hard sand floor. Seagulls nest in the Hall, and their piercing screams and fluttering wings soon drove us out with fingers in our ears. It was a short sail from there to Castle Island, upon which are built great fortifications, now in ruins. Early in the seventeenth century, when the buccaneers made constant raids upon Bermuda, the Government built these great forts, commanding the entrance to the harbor. Once, however, the bold pirates captured the island, and for a long time held the fortifications. The deep paths worn in the coral stone by their heavy boots, as they walked back and forth across the island, can still be seen, now partly hidden from view by waving grasses. Beyond Castle Island are Nonesuch and Cooper Islands. These we passed swiftly, for the wind was fresh, and rounding St. David's Head, a magnificent promontory, against which the waves beat with terrific force, we entered the Narrows and sailed along the coast to St. George's, and finally ended our excursion in the quaint hotel overlooking the bay.

Near St. George's is the Island of St. David's. Every one must go there before he leaves Bermuda, to see the old lighthouse which casts its warning glow over many miles of sea, and to talk with the aged negro, who, with only a solitary donkey for companionship, has never left the little island even to visit St. George's, plainly seen across the water. It is twelve miles from St. George's to Hamilton. The road is as smooth as a floor, now through great walls of solid rock, now along the brilliant sea, and then through groves of palm, cedar and orange-trees. On the way is a place called the Devil's Cave, a fit abode for such monsters, as the ancient readers of Bermudian tales supposed to dwell in these islands. It is a great cave in the rocks, filled with water which runs beneath the island from the sea, rising and falling with the tide. It is alive with groupers whose half human faces are appalling, with small sharks, a devil-fish or two, and schools of angel-fish, looking strangely out of place among "the toilers of the deep."

The coral reefs are full of interest. Williams, a negro of magnificent form and features, who is gaining a wide reputation, knows where the rarest corals lie, and enjoys a coral search as much as the novice. He took me to the inner reefs one day, and with a sea-glass I looked for hours into the blue depths. One can see the bottom of the harbor distinctly beneath forty feet of water in Bermuda, so clear it is, and free from floating weeds and refuse. There were corals in all conceivable forms and shapes; certain growths in the form of elk horns, others in the shape of bells, and huge pieces of brain coral, delicately fashioned, and surrounded by sea-grasses, among which floated fishes of brilliant coloring. Once a huge shark sailed by, guided by a striped pilot-fish, the "sergeant major" of Bermudians; and the angel-fish, radiant with all the colors of the rainbow, swam fearlessly to our boat.

But it is not on the inner reefs that one sees the rarest of the coral formations. Eight or nine miles from shore are the outer reefs, where coral-hunters have not gone, and thither, with pilot Scott of Mangrove Bay, we sailed to see the wonders of the deep. From the yellow beach, past Daniel's Head, ruggedly facing the incessant rush and sweep of the billows, and on and on to the far-away buoy at Chubb's Cut, where lies the channel for ocean steamers. It was smooth and clear that day. Scarcely a ripple stirred the placid ocean, and for an hour or more we looked down upon the most wonderful coral shapes. The sea-urchins and sea-anemones grow there to enor-mous sizes, the former with silvery spines more than a foot in length, protecting the creatures very effectively from the assaults of larger things in search of prey. We wished to stay there until the sun went down; but the islands were so far away that only the white houses could be seen, and they looked like a little Venice in the sea. A strong wind

blew up, the waves grew large and boisterous, and pilot Scott had to stiffen his muscles and beat the water quickly to save our small craft from capsizing. It was dark when we reached Mangrove Bay and crossed Boaz Island, where the steamer was waiting for her evening pas-sengers to Hamilton.

Bermuda contains caves of the most marvelous beauty. None are of great extent; but when one climbs down into the cool depths of Walsingham Cave near St. George's, and lights his cedar boughs beside the underground lake of salt water, he thinks of the wonderful grottoes of Eastern tales. It is still as a dungeon; and the lake, under the light of the blazing boughs, glistens and shim-mers like a great emerald in a setting of the whitest marble. To see one cave is to see them all—Jacob's, Convolvulus and the rest.

The Governor of Bermuda is appointed by the Crown, and the people, under a property qualification, choose a Council and House of Assembly, which meet in a large Government building. Their sessions are long and exciting. Strictly party lines divide the voters, and no American legislator can improvise more flowery and inspiring periods than the assemblyman of the islands. The gover-nor has the power to veto; and after all the talking about popular rights and the terrible corruption of the opposition or the Government, as the case may be, a scratch of his pen settles it. Bermuda is garrisoned by regular troops, and the officers have gay times and nothing to do except at the stated parades. Realiz-ing the importance of the place as a naval station, strict discipline is main-tained among the soldiers, and the forti-fications are always being strengthened and enlarged. The foreign power which attacks the islands will find "a hard nut to crack." The Bermudian people are universally hospitable and courteous, whites and blacks alike. The slaves were emancipated so long ago, that the slave spirit is outgrown, and the negroes have equal rights with the whites, and all citizens respect them. There is no squalid poverty among them, and they are happy and contented, with a bearing very different from that of their fellows in the Southern States.

Bermuda has her pet traditions, and she is very proud of them. Not only did Shakspeare visit her in spirit, but Edmund Waller the poet, and Tom Moore himself once dwelt in the happy islands. Moore was appointed Registrar to the Admiralty and now and then had to try a captured sailor or two, while he prayed and waited for a wár with Spain which was to make him rich and content. Tom Moore led a not unpleasant life in the Islands, but his letters home were full of longing and complaints.

The people were not educated, and knew nothing of dancing, except what might have been taught now and then at long intervals by a stranded dancing master, thrown overboard like Jonah. It is truth to say that the worst of Moore's poems were written in Bermuda; but that is nothing. They were good enough,

and the islands were honored by his presence for about a year, when he tired of his duties, and set sail for New York. He found that city more unbearable than the Summer Isles, and hied himself away to England.

Few people will be as fastidious as the poet; they will find in Bermuda the rarest enjoyment, delighting in the sea and air and sky and earth; with a climate whose restorative powers can scarcely be excelled. There the tired American, weary with the work of trade and offices; weary of the feverish struggle and competition ever going on around him, will find among the cedars of these isles the rest and strength and happiness, which will cause his Bermudian days to be held in blessed remembrance forever.— *Selected.*

Despise not any man, and do not spurn anything; for there is no man that hath not his hour, nor is there anything that hath not its place .

OSTRICHES AT LOS ANGELES.

WITHIN six miles of this beautiful city, on what is known as the old Temple street road, Dr. C. J. Sketchley has started an ostrich farm. He was one of the pioneers in ostrich farming in Africa, where he engaged in the business for many years, and is the author of a number of books on the ostrich and the best methods of ostrich farming. A visit to Los Angeles convinced the doctor that ostrich farming could be successfully carried on there, and he resolved to make the experiment. The result is the Sketchley ostrich farm. On the sixty acres of land devoted to the ostriches there are thirty pairs of these beautiful birds, besides a number of young ones recently hatched.

Their food consists almost wholly of corn and alfalfa, which is a beautiful plant of the Lucerne family. Long experience has shown that this bill of fare will cause the ostrich to produce more feathers and of a better quality than any

other diet. Each male is mated, and the two birds have two acres of ground. The land is fenced off into lots of one acre each. The two birds are kept in one of these lots until they have eaten off all the alfalfa, when they are transferred to the other, being thus alternated between the two. From the observatory tower in the center of the doctor's residence the ostrich grounds look like an immense chessboard, and the gigantic birds like the big pieces scattered over it.

"All the full-grown ostriches you see," said the doctor, "I imported directly from Africa, landing them in this country at Galveston, and bringing with them four Madrasese men and one woman, the people of that tribe being more familiar with the ostrich than any native Africans. Thus far my experience has succeeded beyond my expectations. Not only are ostriches quite as healthy as in Africa, but they are actually more prolific here than in their native country, both in the number of eggs they lay and the number of young ones they hatch, and also in the quantity of feathers they produce—results due, I believe, to this glorious climate, which seems greatly to increase the fertility of all animals. The feathers are fully equal in all respects to any grown in Africa.

"The height of the birds is from eight to twelve feet. Their weight varies from three hundred to four hundred pounds. The male is much the larger, and is black, while the female is gray. Where, then, you will ask, do white ostrich feathers come from? They are found on both the male and female birds among the loose feathers of the wings and tail. It is the fact that they are so much rarer that makes them so much more desired, and, consequently, so much higher in price than black or gray feathers, for in some respects I consider them inferior to the other feathers.

"The female ostrich does not begin to lay eggs until it is four years old, but it produces its first crop of feathers at the end of its first year. Every seven months thereafter its plumage is ready for market, yielding about twenty-five of the very finest feathers, besides a large number of less valuable ones. The feathers are not plucked, but are cut off, quite close to the skin, with large shears made for the purpose. No pain whatever is inflicted in the operation. Within a few days after the feathers have been cut the stubs dry and shrivel to such an extent that they are easily removed. The longest and finest white feathers are worth, wholesale, four dollars apiece, and good feathers are worth two hundred dollars a pound. The first clipping of young birds will average forty dollars in value. Of course, it requires a good deal of capital to start a large ostrich farm, as a full grown pair of birds are worth from seven to eight hundred dollars, and a single young bird six months old costs from one hundred and fifty to two hundred dollars; but after it is once under way, the return from the investment is a large one.

"We very seldom permit the ostriches to do their own hatching, but most of it is performed by incubators. The old idea that ostriches seldom or never require water has long since been proved false. They drink frequently, and even bathe. We keep a water trough in each pen to enable them to do so. No one knows what age an ostrich may attain, but I believe they are next to immortal. In Africa I have seen birds that were known to be over eighty years of age."

I reminded the doctor of a promise he had made to show me a foot race between ostriches. We immediately went to a broad open space between the ostrich pens, and in response to the doctor's call, two superb ostriches came running to him. After caressing the gentle creatures for a few moments he showed them a handful of figs, of which they are extremely fond. Two of his men then restrained the birds by placing nooses about their legs, until he and myself walked away about a quarter of a mile. Then, at a signal from the doctor, the birds were released, and the race began. It was a rare sight. Ornithologists tell us that the stride of the ostrich when feeding is from twenty to twenty-two inches; when walking, not feeding, twenty-six inches; and when terrified, from eleven to fourteen feet. It seemed to me that in this race for a handful of figs from their master, these gigantic birds covered the last-named distance at every stride. Like the wind they came, their great necks stretched forward and upward to their utmost length, and their wings working. They kept well abreast for nearly half the distance, and then one began to forge ahead. He increased his lead till within a short distance of us, when he turned his head, and, seeing that his competitor was considerably in the rear, he slackened his pace, and, jogging up to the doctor, received his reward in figs and caresses. Besides Dr. Sketchley's farm there is another ostrich farm near Anaheim, a thriving town on the Southern Pacific Railroad, twenty-five miles from Los Angeles.

Virtue is like a rich stone, best plain set.—*Lord Bacon.*

THE CLAIMS OF THE ·CATHOLIC CHURCH.

ALL those who profess Christianity, place the foundation of their faith in Jesus Christ. The worship of God is the object which religion proposes to man. Without stopping to consider what man could do, by the unbiased efforts of merely natural reason, to accord proper worship to God, we will start from the fact of Christ's advent among men and His promulgation of the New Law. What do I hold then as a Catholic? What claims does the Roman Catholic Church make? Briefly, these: She claims that Jesus Christ, the second person of the Trinity, is consubstantial and co-equal with His Divine Father: hence, that He is truly God. She claims that He became a true man by assuming our human nature through the conception of the Blessed Virgin Mary, by virtue of the power of the Holy Ghost. Thus that God became man, and was truly born of woman, though no man was His father. His object in thus assuming our nature, was that He might atone for the sins of men, by offering to His Father a sacrifice more than equal to the offence. There were two natures in Christ, distinct and entire, the Human and the Divine; but there was but one person; hence, what he did as man, proceeded from a human nature and a Divine Person. Consequently it was of infinite value.

But how was this scheme of salvation for men to be accomplished? The expiation offered by the Son of God was, if I may use with reverence the expression, the capital which the Christian was to work with. "Faith without works is dead." He uses it by accepting the Revelation which Christ made to men, a Revelation which not only requires the perfect adhesion of the mind by thorough acceptance, but the more important practical acceptance of the heart by conformity of life to its precepts. He taught men not only what they were to believe, but what they were to do. How important it is to know and accept this Revelation and to act up to it is seen from the fact that man's salvation depends thereon.

If we believe in Christ and live up to that belief by our acts, our immortal souls will enjoy the vision of God for all eternity, reaping, namely, the fullest beatitude of which they are capable. If we reject Christ, or accept His teaching, and work sin instead of righteousness, through eternity we shall be separated from Him. Now, if Revelation imports such terrific consequences, if God demands of man belief in certain things and the practice of a virtue consonant with those things, as an essential condition to the attainment of that for which man was created, certainly man has a right to say: "Let me know surely what I am to believe, and what to do; otherwise, God would be treating me, His creature, with revolting unfairness."

Here be it remarked that if one admits Jesus Christ to be God, and to have imparted to men a Revelation of what He requires of their belief, man has no right to ask anything more than to know what the Revelation is. He has no right whatever to examine a point that he knows God to have revealed, in order to see if it be reasonable, or to be accepted. Hence, latitude in religious belief is absurd. There can be no breadth, no latitude. No mathematician can have broad views with regard to the sum of the three angles of a triangle being equal to two right angles. When he has gone through the demonstration, and knows that truth, it is physically impossible for him to hold anything else about that point. If Christ is God, and one knows that He has told him that a thing is true or must be done, it is equally impossible for him to have any opinion or tolerance in regard to that point; therefore, the man who wishes to save his soul must find out what Christ has revealed and commanded, and when he has found that, he has nothing to do except believe it and practice it.

The majority of Christians admit the Divinity of Christ, and claim that they have received His law and wish to practice it. But here again let us suppose a man of good reason, but without any creed, who sees the great number of sects all claiming to have the revelation of Christ, yet teaching contradictory doctrines, and attaching widely different degrees of responsibility to the acceptance of those doctrines; he will reasonably exclaim: "These can not all be right. In fact, if Christ came and made a Revelation, and makes the acceptance of it a condition to salvation, there can be only one that is right—only one that is that Revelation of Christ." Then, if that man were to take a world-wide look at those believers in Christ, he would discover this: He would see millions of men, scattered over every part of the world, who believe one self-same, coherent, homogeneous creed; who claim that they are but the posterity of other millions who believed the same, who, in their turn, had fathers and forefathers, unified by the same creed, and he finds that their belief and their believers reach back to the very time of Christ and His Apostles, as history and tradition will show him. He will see that they all point, and have ever pointed, to a majestic body, which declares to them their belief, guides them in their morals, ministers to them the sacraments. This majestic body is the Church which claims to be authorized by Christ to speak in His name, and, where she acts as His interpreter, to enjoy immunity from error. He sees that this body, which is organic, is over the whole earth, yet subject to one man, who claims to be the successor to the Apostle Peter, in the control of Christendom; namely, he finds that in all times since the advent of Christ, through all parts of the world, among all classes of men, there are millions who profess one faith, under one head, and that this body is and has ever, even among her enemies, been known by the distinctive title of the Catholic Church, viz: The Universal Church.

On the other hand, he sees a great variety of different sects which all profess to exhibit the doctrine of Christ and to be His Church. He sees that they hold views and doctrines different from another, and exhibiting extremes as sundered as Puseyism and Shakerism. He sees they appeal to a book which contains the writings of men, whom Christ chose to do His work, as corroborative of their claims. He looks into the book, and if he were Aristotle himself, he would be unable to tell what it all means; and some parts, very important doctrinally, and which will seem to him to be couched in language, than which no plainer or simpler could be conceived, he will find these sects declaring to not mean what they seem to say. If he is a man of a logical mind, he will say: You all get your doctrines out of this one book, and you all differ, and you all claim to have the right meaning of the book, and yet have no proof to show that you have, and no authoritative tribunal to determine that point. Why, take away that book as a guide. You might as well put a star fish somewhere, with a sign, "Go the way the arms of the fish point." On the other hand, he will see that many things in this book point to just some such body as he has already remarked the Catholic Church to be. He will read there that Christ bade His disciples to go into the uttermost parts of the earth to preach the gospel. He will see that Christ said, "He who heareth you, heareth me, and he who despiseth you, despiseth me." He will see that Christ told them: "I am with you all days, even unto the consummation of the world," and that He declared He would found His church, "against which the gates of hell should not prevail," upon a rock. Moreover, he will find that from the beginning, different bodies have fallen off from the Catholic Church. He will even find that these varying sects of to-day sprang from such a separation from the Church. If he is acquainted with ecclesiastical history, he will see that more than a dozen centuries ago there was a body of Protestants against the Catholic Church, which was more numerous than even the Protestants of to-day. Yet, if he wishes to-day, to find what they taught, he must open the encyclopædia at Arianism or thumb ancient history.

He will, moreover, find that the Catholic or Universal Church is ever strong, prominent and active. Strange, too, he will find that the sects, however much they differ from one another, unite in one thing, viz: in declaiming against this Catholic Church. If he examines the religious bodies that have been formed in this way by receding from the Church, and formulating a creed of their own, he will see that the respective revolting bodies have held different doctrines from each other, while the Church has continued with the calmest tenacity to hold forth the same tenets, and, that never has she retracted or modified a point which she has once declared necessary for belief. What can a logical, philosophical mind, free from all prejudice, think when he considers this fact? Every one who knows the meaning of Truth, knows that Truth is one and immutable, and that Error is as various and changeable as the human mind is protean in its acceptance of opinion.

If in these different revolts from the authority and teaching of the Church, what was lopped from her teachings left a complexus of tenets which were always the same, so that one type, as it were, was ever reproduced and only new assertions to belief were cut off, then there would be strong presumption that the aberrations of human reason, which crept in and corrupted the original deposit of revelation, were periodically corrected by the providence of God, and the pure, simple, homogeneous creed delivered by Christ was restored. But this is not the case. If the sum of the denials of truths taught by the Church were to be made up, one would find that nearly every dogma of the Church had been denied at these different times. Moreover, these different sects have had a disintegration among themselves, and as time went on, either the members of them return to the Church, or lapse into further denial, or theism. Moreover, "by their fruits you shall know them," "A good tree beareth good fruits." There is not a state, not an age, not a condition of man, to which the Catholic Church does not minister spiritually, to which she has not an aid peculiarly adapted. The infant is regenerated and made a child of God by baptism. Those who marry are fortified by a sacrament, and the contract is indissoluble except by death. Those who are Sociologists enough to see that the Family is the foundation of the social fabric will see in this perpetual continuity of the marriage bond a safeguard against the vagaries of passion, the inconsistency of fickle human nature, and the cogent evasion of selfish interests. The divorce courts tell what the opposite doctrine leads to. Those who are the ministers of the Church are consecrated utterly to the service of God. They renounce the joys and consolations of the domestic life, and remain virgins to minister to the Virgin Son of a Virgin Mother.

Again, our calm, cool-headed observer will remark that the founders of the Church were men seemingly the most unqualified for so vast a work of regeneration. They were ignorant, simple, poor, and in the lowest scale of social dignity. They were even, several at least, of weak wills. The doctrines they presented were adverse to the dictates of man's lower nature, they demanded obedience to their teaching as to that of God; they introduced the truest democracy that the world has seen. That little band labored in poverty, and in suffering, and finally laid down their lives in testimony to their faith. Our observer sees the same course followed by the followers of Christ in the Catholic church to-day. His ministers leave all for Him. They penetrate to the remotest lands, suffer every hardship with no temporal gain, and every century sees lives sacrificed on the altar of Catholic faith, through love for the crucified Christ and His own church. One would be justified in concluding, then, that a Church which was precisely what his reason told him the church of Christ ought to be, which for nearly two thousand years has exhibited unswerving fidelity to one creed; which is so manifold in spiritual operations and zeal for souls, so coherent and consistent with herself, so perfectly harmonizing with reason, and which is the very embodiment of what is presented in the Scriptures as the Church; a man free from prejudice, I say, and strong in reason, would be justified in concluding: "If there be a Church founded by Christ, this Roman Catholic Church is it." In fact, many men who desired simply to find the Church of Christ, have sought her and found her by such signs as these. What Justin the Martyr did in the third century Orestes Bronson did in the nineteenth. Each wandered from sect to sect, desirous of truth, and with minds well capable of discerning it. They finally came to the Catholic Church and died in its bosom—stanch exponents of her indubitable claims to the end of their lives.

What then does the Catholic Church teach? She teaches first, that she has been founded by Christ and is the infallible exponent of all that the follower of Christ must believe. She teaches that the teaching of Christ, and hence her teaching, (because she teaches all that Christ taught and nothing but what he taught,) must be accepted, under penalty of losing one's soul if that teaching be rejected. That teaching is summarized thus: Man was elevated in the person of Adam to a supernatural end, viz: he was destined to enjoy, after his probation was over, a knowledge of God, such as God has of Himself, barring the infinite comprehension of the Divine knowledge. He was to merit this end by his deeds. He sinned; and he and, in him, all the human race lost their claim to this supernatural end.

The Word of God, Jesus Christ, God equal to His Father, and to the Holy Spirit, became man of a virgin, who conceived by the power of the Holy Ghost, and without any human instrumentality. This virgin was herself, through exemption, conceived without sin, so that at no moment of her existence was she subject to Satan. This privilege is called the Immaculate Conception. In accordance with her prophecy found recorded in the Inspired Scriptures,—"all generations shall call me blessed,"—all generations do call her blessed, but none save the Catholic generations thus style the Mother of

our Lord the Blessed Virgin. If Protestants use the term, it is to point a sneer at Catholics by it. Every honor, all respect, that can be accorded to a purely human being and a creature, is accorded to her because of her sinlessness, and the incomparable dignity she enjoyed in being chosen by the Eternal Father to be the Mother of His Divine Son, whose human substance was drawn from her pure flesh and blood, which was quickened to the conception of this Divine Son by the agency of the Holy Spirit. The Church teaches that she who was thus honored by God, is powerful with Him to obtain mercy and favor for men; and hence, Catholics supplicate her to intercede for them with God. This is the devotion to the Blessed Virgin put very briefly.

The Church teaches that Christ, by His death on the cross, atoned for the countless sins of men, and heaven, closed by the First Adam, was opened by the Second Adam to mankind. But, as by natural generation men are born to the First Adam, and inherit the nature on which he entailed the loss of heaven, so by spiritual regeneration they must be born children of God, in order to become co-heirs with Christ to the Kingdom of Heaven. Hence, the Church teaches that baptism in water is an essential condition for salvation. Those who are unable to obtain it, but ardently desire it, and feel contrition for their sins, are baptized by this baptism of desire, and those who lay down their lives for Christ, are baptized by a baptism of blood. This three-fold baptism gives the same result—the inheritance of heaven. The soul is cleansed by baptism from all sin.

If man commits a mortal sin, he forfeits the right to the kingdom of heaven. But knowing the frailty of men, Christ instituted another sacrament—that of Penance, or, as it is called, Confession—by which sins committed after baptism are forgiven. All who commit mortal sin after baptism, are bound to confession as the means of release from it, provided by the merciful love of the Redeemer. So far from this holy sacrament being an inducement to sin, it is one of sin's greatest preventives. Every Catholic knows that he cannot obtain the forgiveness of a mortal sin without repenting of it properly, viz: regretting the offense to God, because He is so good, and firmly resolving to avoid all sin in the future. If the priest knows that a sinner has not this purpose in his heart, he also knows that it is vain to give him absolution, because the priest has no power to absolve one not so disposed, and only puts on his own soul the sin of sacrilege by profaning a sacrament. Those who die in mortal sin are damned, viz: they are remitted to a place of eternal punishment. "Depart from me, ye cursed into everlasting fire," Christ will say to the reprobate.

The church teaches that the Eucharist contains the Body and Blood and Soul of Jesus Christ really present, and that after the words of consecration there is no longer aught of bread or wine, except the accidents, *i. e.*, all the phenomena of bread and wine remain without any underlying substance of bread or wine. Christ blessed the bread and said: "This is my body." The Roman Catholic Church believes Him. Some of the disciples said when Christ taught this doctrine: "This is a hard saying; who can hear it?" The Church replies: "I can, because it is my God who utters it." She says with Peter, "Lord, thou hast the words of eternal life—to whom can we go?" If we do not accept what He says, then there is an end to Christian belief, and the question of salvation is over. These are the principal points of the church's doctrine. The celibacy of her clergy is an ecclesiastical dispensation. Christ did not enjoin it. So bestowing communion in one, or in both kinds, is at the option of the church, as is the frequency with which the Eucharist is to be received.

This is a brief *ex pose* of the teachings of the Catholic Church. Her claim to infallibility in her authoritative teaching is the most arrogant pretension ever made by any organization since the world began, if she be not authorized to make that claim, by the sole one who could render her infallible—God. Again if it were man and not God who asserted this, is it possible that through all these centuries she should never have recalled one of her definitions; never have pronounced one that would conflict with another? Think, too, of the millions of secrets that would hopelessly mar reputations that have been poured into the ears of priests in the confessional! Yet although there have been priests who have sunk to the lowest infamy, who have cast their sacerdotal vows to the winds and lived and died libertines and atheists, never has it been known that one of these reprobate pastors has violated the seal of confession and told what had been committed to his confidence in the sacrament of Penance.

Such considerations may well make the serious, earnest seeker after truth inquire if the Catholic Church be not all she claims; whether she be not indeed the spouse of Christ, the one sole representative of God on earth. Many do not care about religion, and infidelity is common among well educated men. Others are so held by the bonds of religious prejudice that they doggedly refuse to examine the claims of the Catholic Church. Others have held out even against the full perception of its truth. Truly, if the Catholic Church be not what she pretends, then would it seem that a human institution has provided better for the needs and desires of mankind than the Almighty has done, and that a human invention exhibits marks that would indicate a Divine character. Take away an infallible authority, and man is at once in the dark as to his most vital necessity—that of securing the blessedness of Eternal Life.

It seems so beautiful and liberal to the unthinking, to say: "Here is God's word; take it, believe it, and practice it." And at the very start, if a man demand, "Prove to me that it is God's word;" the proof cannot be given—and if one knows it to be the word of God, he cannot know what it means. The Bible is enough for the purpose for which it was intended; it is not enough, by itself, for furnishing man with his creed, and the certainty which should accompany his creed. St. Augustine, the greatest intellect since Aristotle, declared he would not believe the Scriptures themselves, unless the Church sanctioned them and vouched for their veracity. We Catholics hold to the Church, the pillar and ground of truth, which, *not* to hear, is to be as a heathen and a publican.

John J. à Becket.

MURDERING GUNS.

THE October issue of *Harper's Monthly* contains an illustrated article by Admiral Simpson of the American navy that deals with the construction of the steel guns, which are to be used to arm the new war ships that Secretary Whitney is going to build. Incidentally the modern machine gun, or quick-firing gun, is mentioned as a "murdering gun," although the article is chiefly devoted to the method of constructing big breech-loaders. A naval officer who talked about these "murdering guns," says:

One has only to stop to think a moment to appreciate the tremendous advance made in the construction of guns during the present century. Every one is familiar with the fact that a very large number of the privateers that did their country such great service in the last war with England were armed with six-pounders— cannon that threw a ball of cast iron weighing six pounds. These guns were mounted in broadside, much as the nine-inch guns on the big wooden frigates, that form the greater part of our navy now, are mounted, and it required about five men to serve them well. They were fired perhaps once in five minutes. Although the principal weapon of the little war ships of twenty-five years ago, the six-pounder is now one of the little guns to be used as the flint-lock muskets were used in those days, to repel attacks from small boats and pick men off exposed parts of an enemy's ship. This latter service gives them the name of murdering guns. The six-pounder of 1812 was usually a brass piece, and the charge of powder was so small that the balls failed often to penetrate the thick plank of an enemy's ship. It is a fact, that, until within forty years, thick timber in the top sides of a ship was a sufficient protection even against the cannon balls of larger degree. But now the quick-firing six-pounder has become an awful weapon of destruction. Its barrel is made of steel. Instead of being fired by touching a flaming match to the priming in the vent of the gun, as the ancient namesake was, it is fired and loaded as well by the motion of a lever. In place of the little loose bag of powder and the round iron ball that loaded the ancient one, a metallic cartridge that is made up of powder fulminate and a long steel bolt is used. The cartridges are placed in a magazine connected with the gun, and the motion of the lever throws out the empty shell after the discharge, inserts a fresh cartridge, and fires it. The speed attained at a recent trial of the Nordenfelt six-pounder at Dartford, England, was six rounds in fourteen seconds. It could be easily and accurately fired twenty times in a minute.

But the speed attained, important as it is, is not the only advantage of these six-pounder quick-firing guns. At the Dartford trial mentioned, the gun was tested to show its power. Five iron plates, each an inch thick, were used over an appropriate backing of wood to form a target, yet the steel bolts which this gun threw, with such marvelous rapidity passed clear through the five inches of iron plates, the gun being fired at a distance of sixty yards from the target. That is the sort of weapon that the thin racing shells called torpedo boats have got to face. The little steamer may fly at a speed of twenty-five miles an hour, but unless she can get unobserved within a very short distance of the big man-of-war she seeks to destroy, the captain will get the range of her with the lightning six-pounders, and before she can travel three times her length will drive such a shower of steel bolts clear through' hull, boiler, and everything about her that not a soul nor a fragment will be left above water, to tell whence she came or mark where she went down. Not even the best of torpedo boats, except through an accident of fog or in smoke of battle between larger ships, can hope to reach an enemy to do him hurt.

One glory of naval warfare has departed forever—the glory of laying a ship yard-arm to yard-arm beside the enemy, and to the mad music of the ratchet, with sword and pike swarming over the rail and sweeping the enemy from his own deck. It can not be done now because sailormen do not fight on open decks. The six-pounder is the slowest of the machine guns, and in the matter of destroying men who are unprotected by shields of metal the least effective. Quick-firing guns that throw projectiles the size of a rifle ball are made in great variety. The single-barrel Nordenfelt of this calibre weighs but fifteen pounds, and can be fired one hundred and eighty times a minute. The next larger size has three barrels. It weighs sixty pounds and can throw four hundred projectiles a minute. This is just now a very popular weapon in the French, German, and Italian armies, both on account of its effectiveness and the lightness in weight. It is mounted on a light carriage for field service. On ship board, however, the five-barrel gun is the smallest size used. Larger ones, having ten barrels, weighing two hundred and twenty pounds, have been devised for use in forts as well as on ships, and even twelve-barrel guns that weigh two hundred and sixty pounds are becoming common. The ten-barrel gun throws one thousand pro-

jectiles a minute, and the other one thousand two hundred. Their effective range is a little over one thousand yards. One gun like this is warranted to keep the open ports of an enemy's ship clear when within range.

A curious test was made with one of the ten-barrel guns not long ago in India. Two companies of wooden soldiers were set up on the rifle range. A company of fifty men, armed with the best modern rifles, fired at one of the companies of wooden targets at a distance of one thousand yards, while a ten-barrel machine gun peppered the other company during the same interval of time. It required six men to feed, aim, and fire the machine gun. An examination of the targets showed that the machine gun did as much work as the fifty trained men. But in time of actual battle the trained men, owing to the excitement and fatigue incident to the contest, could not fire with the accuracy nor speed attained in a practice drill at a mark, while the machines, having neither nerves nor muscles would spout death with unvarying accuracy and speed. It is no longer possible to work a cannon on an unprotected deck, except when out of range of the murdering guns of the enemy. It is not possible to take an enemy's ship by boarding. Small boats can never hope to carry an enemy's ship by pouring a host of men on her deck, nor can torpedo boats approach within torpedo range except by stealth. Naval warfare is being narrowed down pretty well to contests between ships at long range with guns of immense power. A knowledge of mathematics, chemistry, and mechanics is now as necessary for a modern naval seaman, as courage and seamanship were to naval seamen of seventy-five years ago.

THE MOREKIDITES MUST GO.

TWELVE hundred years hence, in the year of our Lord 3100, there dwelt on the banks of the Athabasca River, in the Territory of Athabasca (then a satrapy of the United States; now a part of British America), a people, who were called peculiar. They had earned this designation because they differed from the rest of the civilized world in their marriage customs. It will be remembered that at that day, nations most advanced in culture, had, for reasons that will be stated in the course of this narrative, ceased to permit more than one child to a family. It was, therefore, in defiance of popular customs that some thirty years before the time mentioned above, a people, who were called the Morekidites, went forth into the northern wilderness, and, under the plea of religion, organized their families on the polykid basis.

They boldly preached that there was nothing wrong in having more children than one, and as boldly carried this novel doctrine into practice; so that, while among the civilized peoples of the earth, no family could be found in which there was more than one child, there existed on the Athabasca, whose austere banks they had made to blossom as the rose, this peculiar sect, with families containing, many of them (Shades of the Sainted Edmunds!) as many as six, ten, and even twelve children.

Well, this had gone on for a great many years before Congress paid any attention to it; but finally, after a generation had passed away, that august body awakened to a realization of the growing evil, and in accordance with their gray haired prerogative of robbing the hen roosts of the Territories with impunity, passed drastic measures against the Morekidites; made it a felony to have a second child, and a misdemeanor to "hold such a child out to the world." (Note: The law read as quoted, and being ambiguous as to whether physical or other holding was meant, gave ample opportunity for the courts to drive whole wagon-loads, cart-loads and dray-loads of decisions through it.)

Now, these laws were being vigorously enforced; carpetbagging officials, supposed to be either dishonest or incompetent, having been induced to leave settled practices at middle-age, to accept small salaries in a distant territory, were substituting frenzy for zeal, and prejudice for law. Arrests were made daily; penitentiaries were teeming, and the charge of bastardy rested upon four-fifths of the children of the community; strange events of the saddest nature were of frequent occurrence. The people could have stood all this—religion would have nerved them up to even more—had they been spared one cruel blow, they and the Almighty, who was fighting their battle, might have succeeded ultimately—but that blow fell—then perished hope. I refer to the organization of the regenerators of Athabasca—the Young Democracy. Strong men became weak, when they heard it; women shed tears of blood, and the stoutest hearts quailed.

Just previous to the events narrated in this historical sketch, John Anderson McAnderson of Andersonville had been duly indicted by a grand jury of his peers; twenty-four trustworthy gentlemen, so patriotic that they sought rather than avoided the service of their country amidst the dangers of the court room, for the paltry consideration of a dollar and a half a day, which they scorned, yet accepted. Now these particular twenty-four grand jurors had been brought in from the penitentiary, on open venire, to sit as inquisitors upon the Morekidites, since it was a requirement of law that no one connected with that peculiar sect should be permitted to act as jurors on their trials. It so happened that, except the imported office holders, there were no dissenters from the Morekidites in the land, save it were in the penitentiary, and there the population was entirely made up of dissenters—therefore juries, grand and petit, came from that public institution. And when on various occasions learned counsel had objected that it was infamous to entrust convicts with such important and delicate duties, his honor, Judge Orthodox Ranter, had promptly overruled the objection with the statement, that this method of selecting jurors brought to the service of the government, a class of profoundly experienced men, who, it was true, he admitted, were temporarily under a cloud, but who had during their residence in the public prison, been exemplary in conduct; he defied (whereupon he struck the desk a heavy blow) any man to allege a single case of malfeasance against one of the gentlemen concerned during the period of their incarceration—they had been uniformly honest, uniformly sober, uniformly obedient, and were home and in bed early every night. When learned counsel ventured to suggest that compulsion had accomplished this wonderful reformation, his Honor, with an oath in Norman-French, which his less learned auditors supposed to be a quotation from Blackstone, fined the counsel two hundred dollars, and said that as long as his country willed, nay, insisted that he preside in the Eleventh District Court, he would permit no attorney to push a reforming man back into depths from which he, with so much trouble, had dragged himself. "Otherwise," he remarked, "where were the incentive to reform?" Tow hich no one replied.

Well, the day of the trial came on. Mr. Setemup, the district attorney, proceeded to empanel the jury. The usual number of convicts were brought in and duly questioned as to their past record. The district attorney promptly challenged all those who had not served at least two previous terms of imprisonment, on the ground that they were without experience in jury trials. Challenge sustained. The attorney for the defense made a score of objections which were promptly overruled; and finally interposed an objection to the entire jury; whereupon the Court, after a fit of coughing which continued for five minutes, informed the counsel, that their point had been expressly decided by the Court, a hundred times; that it could only be viewed in the light of intended disrespect that it was again urged; that a repetition would be followed by disbarring and the appointment of a commission of lunacy to inquire into his apparently desolate mental condition. The attorney took an exception to such language, which was promptly overruled.

McAnderson was then arraigned upon one indictment for polykidamy, or having more children than one; and another indictment for holding the child out to the world as his own—which latter had thirty-one counts. It may readily be

imagined that the position of the defendant was anything but agreeable, with an aggregate imprisonment of twenty years and six months and an aggregate fine of over ten thousand dollars staring him in the face. But the reader must understand that the government meant business; there was to be no trifling; this community was to be reformed and reformed immediately. In vain had the friends of this persecuted sect pointed out that great bodies move slowly; that social revolutions require time.

McAnderson pleaded not guilty, and Mr. Setemup had risen to his feet, and was about to make his opening address, when Bill Sykes, the foreman of the jury, rose from his chair, and addressing the court, said: "If your honor please, we've talked this case over among ourselves, and havin' a good deal of confidence in the commissioner who held the prisoner to await the action of the gran' jury, and also in the gran' jury who indicted him, we've come to the conclusion that there aint any doubt of his bein' guilty, and so we return a verdic' of guilty."

It is needless to relate that the judge and the district attorney nearly expired in their places; the occurrence was, in the slang of the day, such a "dead give away." It suggested that the scales of justice, which ought to indicate every grain, were soldered at the pivot. The court officers did considerable humming and hawing, but finally, the district attorney seizing the reins, reminded the jury that the forms of justice must be preserved, that the sacred provisions of the Constitution must not be rudely thrust aside.

McAnderson's counsel promptly objected to the jury, on the ground of prejudice, saying that "it is evident to the meanest understanding" that his client was even then convicted, and a trial would be but a farce, before that jury. The district attorney replied that Webster defined prejudice to be an "unreasonable predilection for or against," and, he said, "Is my opponent prepared to say that the conclusion reached by the jury, was without reason? Are not the facts that the commissioner held the defendant, and that the grand jury indicted him, reason? Are those officials in the habit of holding innocent people? Therefore, their judgment is not unreasonable, and therefore not prejudice." Overruled. Exception taken—noted.

The district attorney then delivered his address—outlined the charges against the defendant, and the line of proof.

The first witness called by the prosecution, was Sarah McAnderson, the wife of the defendant. Counsel for the defense promptly arose and delivered an argument against compelling a wife to testify against her husband; quoting a line of authorities and precedents as far back as the ancient Greenleaf. But the objection was overruled, after the argument of Mr. Setemup, who contended that the law, which he read, expressly stated that a husband should not be a witness for or against his wife, nor a wife a witness for or against her husband, except, and, "mark the exception," he said, "in an action or proceeding by one against the other. Now, your honor, who are the parties to this action? Is it not the people against McAnderson? It is, I unhesitatingly reply. And, what people, your honor? *The* people, the whole people of Athabasca—every other person in this Territory of the United States, besides the defendant. And in this enumeration is included, must be included, the wife of the defendant. Therefore I contend that she is brought plainly under the exception and that she must be compelled to testify, being a party plaintiff and her husband being the party defendant. The counsel for the defense denounced this as a monstrous proposition, and argued that in a course of fifteen centuries, this point had never been raised, which is convincing proof that it is unreasonable and untenable.

The Court announced that he would hold the point under advisement for seven minutes, and granted a recess for that length of time. His Honor disappeared through a side door into an adjoining saloon, where authorities in such deep subjects were found in the bottom of a glass of Old Rye, but for some reason, the first authority was not satisfactory and another was consulted, which seemed to clear up any lingering doubt that remained, and His Honor found his way back to the court room, having consumed, to the second, the seven minutes allowed,—he had been there before. Resuming his seat, he remarked, by way of preface, that he had, to brush aside a lingering doubt, consulted several leading ornaments of the bar, of ancient reputation, profound and inspiring. After which he overruled the objection of the defense and permitted the witness to testify. She was the lawful wife of the defendant and the so-called mother of the infant— which was produced and marked "Exhibit A." Was not really the mother of the child, which had been left on her doorstep. Believed in polykidamy; that it was right. It may be remarked, in passing, that the district attorney afterwards commented upon the deplorable perjury of the witness, Sarah McAnderson, in alleging that the child was left upon her doorstep, and observed, that although the defense had endeavored to prove it by offering a dozen witnesses, they had failed to bring the only witness the Court would permit to testify on the subject—the person who left the child on the doorstep. He asserted that an oath had no binding force on a Morekidite, and that perjury was a part of their education.

The prosecution continued by showing the age of the infant; which was done by calling in a veterinary surgeon to look at its teeth. He pronounced the child to be three years and eleven days old, or since the indictment had been procured fifteen days before, two years, eleven months and twenty-six days at the time of the filing of the indictment. This, of course rendered the defendant liable to punishment under the more serious charge. The thirty-one counts of the lesser indictment were severally proven by evidence of the purchase of paragoric, a rattle, a bolt of diapering, a paper of safety pins, etc.; by evidence that at two o'clock in the morning, the shadow of the defendant with an infant in his arms was cast on the window shade; that the child from its earliest talking called him "papa," and so on *ad thirty-one-dum.*

For the defense, the counsel offered to show that the defendant had been in Europe constantly for two years before the birth of the child. The Court, at a hint from Mr. Setemup, made the following remarks: "It is the chief glory of the common law that it is flexible, adapting itself to changing times and circumstances. It is judge–made law; the outgrowth of the necessities of a free people, where statutes fall short of a complete system of justice. Where great wrongs have required great remedies, the flexibility, the adaptability of the common law, has been equal to the occasion —and such has been the case, even if time honored precedents have been departed from and disputed. The violations of law in this community, not being sporadic, but organized, the wrong is stupendous, the remedy must be radical. It has been an indisputable presumption of law that if a husband has been in the country of his wife and home, he is the father of her child; or, in other language, that he must·be presumed to be the father, if it has been possible for him to be so. The time has come to forsake precedent, to widen the presumption, and therefore, it is my opinion that unless the defense can show that the defendant was beyond the earth, or dead, it is an incontestable presumption that he is the father of the child.". Counsel for defense took an exception; the court fined him twenty-five dollars for contempt.

The evidence being submitted, the court crier went around and woke up the eleven jurymen who were asleep— the other was obstinate and showed a strong desire to do his duty, which the prosecution took as an indication that he would fail to agree; that he was one of the finical "cusses," too particular by half—but after all, he was all right; it was the toothache that gave him the wide awake, conscientious appearance.

The district attorney, Mr. Setemup, then began his closing address to the jury. It was pronounced a masterly effort, evincing deep philosophical research. He said: "Gentlemen of the jury, your honor, ladies and gentlemen: Is the condition of the world, to-day, better than fifteen centuries ago? Without hesitation, with emphasis, I assert that it is. We must look to history for the cause. Nor will the cause be found in modern history; we must search back into those ages, when society, that she might exist, cut from her frame, the ulcer that threatened her existence. And in order that it may be the more apparent that such heroic treatment wrought the cure, we will glance back, cursorily, into the times, beyond which history does not instruct us. Following the scriptural account, we assume that once man and his companion dwelt upon this vast earth, alone; but the species multiplied, and by means of polygamy, soon filled up the land of its inception—overflowing. New lands were settled, and thus swelled the tide of humanity, until the known world was crowded. And in the earliest days, land being unbounded, the subsistance of the human being came from the pursuit of grazing; with increased numbers, came necessity of agriculture; with the more dense population of succeeding ages, came the necessity of manufacture. Thus man adapted himself, both in the search for new lands, and in the invention of new methods of manufacture, to the necessities of changing circumstances. But inevitably in each locality there came the day, when goaded on by the jarring interests of a dense population, neighbor arose in contention against neighbor; city arose in warfare against its neighboring city; wars of conquest became frequent, and as the demand, created by the increase of population, became large compared with the supply, misery in the various forms of poverty, disease, death, in the horrors of warfare, stalked through the land. It was the offspring of polygamy; but, fortunately, as long as unsettled countries and undiscovered mines existed, there yet remained a remedy—for the abundance of nature supplied the needs of the human race.

"Along about the Christian era, the

Romans, the most enlightened people of the earth, abandoned plural marriage, and soon monogamy became the rule of civilized nations. This was a timely check to the growing evil; but even monogamy itself was then an evil; and then, in addition, it was a fraction of the world only, who had abandoned polygamy. The discovery of America was a fortunate event, giving room for the overflowing nations of the east to seek homes in the pristine wilds of a new hemisphere. This was however but a temporary relief; it was not long before the evils of over-population brought suffering to the people of the entire world. It appalls the imagination to contemplate the miseries of ten and twelve centuries ago. There was poverty with its train of evils—starvation, cold, disease, ignorance. It is fortunately beyond the scope of the imagination of our happy age to picture the evils of the crowded cities of that time—the towering tenements, families of ten living in a single room, with no furniture, and with rags, garnered from the streets as bedding. The world was degenerating; poverty was increasing and ignorance; and it was a marked fact that where families were largest, where populations were most dense, there were found poverty and ignorance in its superlative degree. Misery came thereby not only to the individual but likewise to society. Secret crimes increased—anarchy, communism, socialism, nihilism were rife—the earth was not free from wars nor rumors of war.

"It was then in the middle of the twentieth century, that the courageous band of philosophers and statesmen, arose in our fair land, who attributed, correctly, the evils of the times to over population, and who, with consummate boldness and energy, sought in legislative enactment the remedy of the wrong. It was, then, our magnificent country that led the van in the curative movement. It was with some difficulty that the new statutes were enforced; but the good sense of the succeeding generations saw the wisdom of the law that prescribed that there should be but one child to the family. The civilized nations of Europe soon followed and to-day and for eight long centuries back it has been the rule of the enlightened of the earth that but a single child should be permitted. Being a rule founded in the good of mankind, it is regarded as a rule of virtue. And there is no need for men to inform this intelligent jury that the violation of this ancient custom is regarded as a breach of morality, a wrong in itself, a *malum in se.* Nor need I remind you of the results of this happy rule. Populations have been less dense; comfort has taken the place of poverty; enlightenment, of ignorance; private broils and public brawls are of the rarest occurrence.

"Now gentlemen, shall we permit these deluded, shall I say licentious, people to set up a system here which shall overturn the happy work of centuries, and bring to us the days of ten centuries ago? God forbid! It shocks the moral sense of our age; it is an offense that smells to heaven. Think, gentlemen of the jury, think of the consequences of such a system; of the jealousies that would be introduced into a family by having more than one child. They can not tell us that parents love one child as another. It is impossible. They would love one beyond another, and then they introduce into the holy precincts of the family jealousy and discord. The means that now go to educate one, to surround him with the comforting and elevating influences of a luxurious home, would dissolve in necessities, and how long would it be before we would be dragged back into the barbarism of old. Nor can this misguided people be permitted to flaunt, in the face of society, the opportunities of their polykid families. Nor, to plead revelation as the moving principle of their licentious, infamously immoral practices. They are opposed to the sentiments of the age; they outrage every principle esteemed as holy by our enlightened people. They must go; and, gentlemen, as it is the province of a jury to echo the morality of their times, I confidently expect you to do your duty in the case at bar."

Opposing counsel then replied. He ridiculed the assertion of Mr. Setemup that over-population had been responsible for the ills of mankind, which he attributed to the selfishness and wickedness of the world, and asserted that, on the other hand, the District Attorney had made it evident to his auditors that advancement from grazing to agriculture, and from agriculture to manufacture, and thus on to the perfections of civilization, had been due to the fact that the necessities of increasing population had begotten superior intelligence from age to age; that the times of least population, due to the ease of existing, were times of least intelligence; and he asked: "Is it not probable that the tendency now is deterioration?" He suggested that the days of greatest distress were the days of most prolific invention; that to the centuries where poverty was most general are to be attributed the invention of the railroad, the telegraph, the ocean steamship, the telephone and the thousand other applications of electricity. He argued that even admitting that the ultimate results of old systems would be the crowding of the earth, that it might be possible, certainly that was the belief of his client, that the Almighty might choose to raise up a righteous seed unto Himself, in which event the multiplication of such a seed would be right, no matter what might be said of the rest of the world. He said that such considerations would suggest that the prevailing moral sense of civilized nations, which was shocked at the family customs of the Morekidites, was based not so much upon reason as upon the *ex cathedra* decrees of tradition.

A glance back at the varying marriage customs of the ages, would show us that moral sense changes from time to time, and "Were it not presumptuous in us," he said, "to criticize the morality of the age that produced an Abraham, a Moses, that made adultery punishable by stoning to death, that closed the mouth of our Savior against the marriage customs of his own and the patriarchal age; to criticize the morals of the great reformers, who were monogamists in the old sense,

and some of whom, sanctioned the morality of polygamy. The assertion that these were ancient times does not meet the point; since if it were assumed that virtue comes with intelligence we should look for the upper strata of society, the educated and enlightened, to surpass in virtue their less favored contemporaries—while the contrary is notoriously the case. And again, we would expect to find the intelligent nations, those in the vanguard of civilization, more moral, possessing a higher moral sense than the barbarous and semi-barbarous nations of the world. But, we find statistics will demonstrate that the contrary is the case—that we can find no barbarous country that presents a condition so appalling as some of the European nations, where a quarter of the births are outside of legitimate wedlock. Are we then in a position to hold up our hands in holy indignation at the morals of this community, being ourselves poisoned through and through with poisons of immorality, while every authority bears record of the fact that this sect is singularly free from sexual sins and that the adulterer can have no place among them? I, for one, bow my head in reverence to their superior morality. Let not the age, the people, that licenses prostitution, and revels in the evils of illicit intercourse, cast a stone at the age, or the people, who live in a moral righteousness. Would not a man be a hypocrite, who would exact of others that which he scorns himself? Is not a nation, a generation of hypocrites, which, being steeped in licentiousness, punishes a people of superior morality for a fancied evil?"

The judge charged the jury in his usual style; had something to say about the five hundred millions of people in this glorious country being shocked, and being in earnest, called the defendant hard names, and in one of his more forcible strictures threw an inkstand at the defendant, which nearly brained him, and wound up by dancing a frenzied jig on the judicial rostrum. The jury then retired, sought the judicial bar-room, ordered twelve deep potations, agreed that any man who failed to drink voted not guilty, and drank unanimously to the health of the defendant. They came into court and delivered their verdict.

Upon sentencing the prisoner, the judge remarked that there was an ancient Arizona precedent, for trying a man under one statute and sentencing him under another, that, therefore, he would sentence the prisoner for horse stealing, the penalty being the more severe.

Thus ended the trial of John Anderson McAnderson, in which the great government of the United States was the party plaintiff.   *Samuel Sorghum.*

COMMENTS OF THE DAY.

So many dangers beset the walks of Saints that signals are required for their preservation. The ministers of life selected by the Lord and entrusted with the care of His people in this dispensation, have done well their part in notifying the latter of the pitfalls that are open for them. If the warning of the past were sufficient to save the people, writing and preaching for that purpose would no longer be needed. But new members are gathered in, and they with the youth in Zion, need the same signals that have done such good service in the past. Then those who have been warned are forgetful and become careless, and incline to treat lightly the lessons of the past, in some instances, and require constant reminding.

The unequally yoking together of believers with unbelievers is a great danger threatening the Latter-day Saints. The daughters of Zion are more inclined to make this mistake than her sons. But in olden times history testifies the reverse to have been the rule. The men of Israel were condemned frequently for marrying strange women. Now the Lord has gathered His people by the preaching of the Gospel to this choice land, to educate them and to raise up a righteous seed that will hear Him and do His will. He has given us one faith and one spirit. He has called us out of and to be separate from the world; from their ways and from their spirit. Our gathering and coming out from the world would be in vain, if we were to mix and mingle with the world in marriage and all their ways as before. We cross the danger line if we engage in any manner, in ways the Lord designed us to avoid, when He gathered us out.

When a daughter of Zion marries an unbeliever she separates herself from her family, from the Saints, from the ordinances of the Gospel, and consequently from the fellowship of the Holy Ghost. She deprives herself of family prayers, her children are not heirs of the New Covenant, and they are deprived of the Patriarchal blessings and instructions that the children of Saints are entitled to. Chances are largely against their ever embracing the Gospel, and if they do not, they fall into line against the Kingdom of God. Thus the sins of the parents fall upon posterity, and the consequential damages are greater than we can estimate. There is also danger of contamination of other branches of the family by communication and association. Strange men and women lead away the hearts of the sons and daughters of Zion after idols, and from the true and living God. There can be no harmony and but little peace' in such a family unless the believer deserts the faith and cuts loose entirely from allegiance to the Gospel. If there is not union in the household, contentment and happiness are gone. No daughter of Zion should receive the attentions and give encouragement to an unbeliever. It is a sure sign of weakness of faith; and the same is true in regard to the sons of Zion.

Isaac and Rebekah had the correct feeling upon this subject, and their minds were full of grief when Esau took Hittite women of the land to wife. Gen. xxvi. 34, 35. "And Rebekah said to Isaac, I am weary of my life because of the daughters of Heth: If Jacob take a wife of the daughters of Heth, such as these which are daughters of the land, what good shall my life do me?" Gen. xxvii. 46. The course of Father Abraham, when he was near his death, as recorded in Gen. xxiv, is the strongest lesson on record of the importance of proper marriages. He called to him his eldest servant who ruled over all he had, and said to him: "Put, I pray thee, thy hand under my thigh, and I will make thee swear by the Lord, the God of heaven, and the God of the earth, that thou wilt not take a wife unto my son, of the daughters of the Canaanites, among whom I dwell: but thou shalt go unto my country, and to my kindred, and take a wife unto my son Isaac." And the servant put his hand under the thigh of Abraham, his master, and sware to him concerning that matter. We find this servant, under this solemn oath and charge, fitting up for his journey of several hundred miles from Hebron in Judea, to Nahor in Mesopotamia, with ten camels; and a very important lesson is taught us in the operation of this trusted man, for he conversed with the Lord, asking Him to overrule and arrange the approach of the damsel, that he should know her. The Lord sent Rebekah so that she was readily recognized by the servant.

How many of the young men and maidens of Latter-day Israel have had such vigilance exercised over them, in regard to making their selection of husbands and wives? I fear that gross negligence is chargeable to parents in Zion on this score and undying sorrows entailed upon families. This great danger would be still more frequently met with, if we were to allow our children to be taught by imported teachers. The spirit of the Gospel revolts at the approach of all such dangers, while the spirit of the world is eager to have us embrace them. This is one sign by which we may know the spirit of the Lord. I have never known the contrast between it and that of anti-Christ more plainly exhibited, than in the camp-fires of the G. A. R., held in Salt Lake City during the past summer. They exhibited the same spirit of murderous diabolism that has

sacrificed the lives of the innocent in all ages, and that invented the tortures which man has endured from his brother.

Do Latter-day Saints wish to be baptized with that spirit? Oh no! It is the spirit of the evil one, that takes men down to the pit. It should be shunned as the gates of hell. In absence of other friends, the spirit of the Lord will always raise a danger signal for us when one is needed; therefore to retain this spirit and to become acquainted with its operations, is a most important duty.

Proper and timely danger signals should be raised by all parties who have the care of souls; and thus relieve themselves of responsibility, and be saviors indeed to those whom God has entrusted to their care. There is danger of fathers being too reticent with their families. I have known men, who were ministers of the Gospel, to spend a great deal of time with their children, but would never speak to them upon the principles of the Gospel, nor teach them to pray. They appeared to think their public teachings were all sufficient and, in order that the praying should be well done, they would do it all themselves; thus letting their children, grow up in theological idleness. Parents should converse freely with their children upon every principle of life, that they may early understand them and practically demonstrate their truth and power. Under the influence of the Holy Spirit every child should be converted to the truth, by the teachings of its parents. Parents should be good authority to their children, and should be competent to teach them the principles of the Gospel, as early as they can receive them. Then all the additional light they can get from public instructions, sabbath schools, improvement associations and from private individuals, as well as from reading good books, will tend to strengthen the faith and enlarge the understanding and confirm the doctrines planted in them by their parents. Children are entitled to benefit by what their parents know, in regard to religious as well as secular affairs; and how can they profit unles they be taught?

There is danger in backbiting, tale-bearing and evilspeaking. I know of nothing of an ordinary nature that will sooner disturb or offend the Spirit of the Lord than speaking evil of neighbors; speaking of and sometimes exaggerating their faults. It is a grievous sin, and when it is indulged in, where the Spirit of the Lord is, it will surely be rebuked or the spirit will be withdrawn. We should cultivate the habit of speaking of our neighbor's virtues, and if we talk of their vices let it be to them, with the view of making reformation.   *F. M. Lyman.*

BURDEN OF WELSH FARMERS.

THE average American farmer loves a tax bill about as well as a black snake. He ought, therefore, to have a sympathetic feeling for his Welsh brethren, who are just now savagely fighting the church tithe system. An aggravating feature of this tax is that it is collected for the support of clergy of the Church of England, while three-fourths of the tax payers are dissenters. The tithe is levied on all produce of land, while other forms of property are exempt. In England and Wales two-thirds of the land is subject to this impost, the other third being ancient church property whose tithes were long ago merged with the rents. Till the year 1836 the tithe was taken in kind. The parson was entitled to each tenth bundle of wheat or barley, each tenth cock of hay, each tenth calf, and foal, and lamb, and pig, each tenth swarm of bees, in fact the tenth of every-thing down to kitchen herbs. The farmer could not store his wheat or hay, rain or shine, till after proper notice was given to the clergyman, who was on hand to pick out his dues. Some of the inconveniences of this system were abated by agreements to pay in money, and in 1836 a law was enacted making all tithes collectable in this form.

Estimates of the value of the chief crops were based on average prices for seven years, one year being knocked off and a new one added each season. For the greater part of the time the clergy have had the best of the bargain, though when the gold discoveries in California and Australia brought prices up, they depressed the value of the tithe. This now stands at ten per cent. below par; that is, that which at one period went as high as one hundred and eleven pounds now rests at ninety pounds. But, to compensate for this, farm produce has fallen, while farm labor has gone up, so that to-day the tithe is an intolerable burden to the Welsh farmer. It is no less grievous in England, but the aver-age agriculturist there is a good church-man, and pays his tithe with a similar fervor, though somewhat cooled · no doubt, with which he reads his prayers. The best obtainable figures give the amount thus collected in England and Wales as nearly twenty million dollars yearly. That is, indeed, something to whistle over.

And the Welsh farmers are whistling a lively tune about this time. Their land-lords have reduced rents from ten to even fifty per cent. in some cases, but the clergy are firm. The farmers refuse to pay. Then come seizures and sheriffs' sales. The farmers club together and abstain from bids. They boycott auc-tioneers and sheriffs. But the law is too much for them. They are patient, how-ever, and up to now they abstain from violence. But the agitation has spread, and the quarrymen and coal miners have recently joined the farmers. It is a pretty quarrel, and if John Bull does not withdraw his atttention from India and Egypt a bit and take a sympathetic peep at the Welsh farmers, he is likely some day to have a second Ireland on his hands.

HOW TO MAKE STEEL STOLEN.—A little more than a hundred years ago the manufacture of steel had a beginning in England, and about that time there was living in Sheffield a man by the name of Huntsman. · He was a watch and clock maker, and he had so much trouble in getting steel that would answer for his springs he determined to make some himself. · He experimented for a long time, and after many failures hit upon a process that produced a very fine quality of steel. The best steel at that time was made by the Hindoos and it cost in

England about fifty thousand dollars a ton; but Huntsman could make his for five·hundred dollars a ton. He therefore found a ready market for all the steel he could make, and determined to keep his invention secret, and no one was allowed to enter his works except his workmen, and they were sworn to secrecy. Of course, other iron and steel makers were very desirous of finding out how he produced the steel he made, and accomplished it at last: One dark and cold winter night a wretched looking beggar knocked at the door of Huntsman's works and asked shelter from the storm that was raging without. The workmen kindly gave him permission to come in and find warmth and shelter near one of the furnaces. In a little while the drowsy beggar fell asleep, or seemed to do so, but beneath his torn and shabby hat his half-shut eyes watched with eager interest every movement made by the men about the furnaces, and as the charging of the melting pots, heating, and at last pouring the steel into ingots took several hours, it is hardly necessary to add that the forgotten beggar slept long, and, as it seemed, soundly, in the corner where he lay. It turned out afterward that the apparently sleeping beggar was a well-to-do iron maker living near by, and the fact that he soon began the erection of large steel works similar to Huntsman's was good evidence that he was a poor sleeper but a good watcher.

THINK OF IT!—The following diagram represents in round numbers sundry yearly expenditures by the people of the United States. It compares the cost of their vices with their expenditures for the necessaries of life, and sharply defines the interest of the people at large, in the things that relate to the welfare of society.

Alcoholic Liquors, $900,000,000.
Tobacco, $690,000,000.
Wool, Cotton and Sugar, $602,000,000.
Iron, Steel and Lumber, $523,000,000.
Bread, $505,000,000.
Meat, $303,000,000.
Public Education, $92,000,000.
Home and Foreign Missions, $5,500,000.

With the above figures before us can we wonder at the crime, social disorder, domestic unhappiness, sickness and sorrow that abound in the land? Truly they indicate a standard of morality, of which the nation might well take heed, when deliberating upon drastic measures for the correction of its best citizens, whose proportionate responsibility for the condition above shown is less than that of any other people of the Republic.

ONE AUTUMN DAY.

One autumn day the sun shone clear and bright,
  O'er hill and meadow, field and silent wood,
Where oft in childhood sunny hours took flight,
  In weaving flowers in wreaths as best I could.

The sky was lovely in its perfect blue;
  So soft, so tranquil in the radiant light,
The clouds like heavenly beings seemed imbued
  With power to reach the land of spirits bright.

The air was filled with odors rich and rare,
  Of flowers whose beauty graced sweet Woodlawn's shade,
Their gay bright petals soon were left to die,
  Beside the brooklet in the meadow dale.

The day was fair, the birds sang merrily;
  Each to another would his joy impart;

There could be seen the sere and yellow leaves,
That rustled when the faintest breeze would start.

That autumn day in memory's archive dwells;
  Its scenes shall unforgotten ever be;
In dreams I wander back to shady dells,
  Where cuckoo builds his nest among the trees.

One autumn day before its quiet close,
  Sweet Lillie's spirit took its upward flight;
We laid her gently where the violet grows,
  And moonbeams shed their pale, cold shadowy light.

O Lillie! I shall meet you soon I know!
  This earthly pilgrimage will soon be o'er;
O then what joy, what love will fill my soul!
  When I shall meet you on the golden shore.

Minnie.

THE CONTRIBUTOR.

JUNIUS F. WELLS, Editor.

PUBLISHED BY THE CONTRIBUTOR COMPANY.

Terms: Two Dollars a Year, in advance.

SALT LAKE CITY,   DECEMBER, 1886.

SYSTEM IN THE ASSOCIATIONS.

THE longer the Improvement Associations live the more apparent does it become that a systematic order of exercises is necessary to secure the best results. Where there is no regular order of exercises, the meetings become mere entertainments for an hour, and programme committees are charged with the the duty of varying them from week to week, so that they will "draw" large audiences. In some places this appears to be the leading consideration in preparing the programmes. We have always thought this idea to be an erroneous one and regret that the disposition to pander to it is so widespread. We are striving in the Associations for substantial results. Our mission is to convert the young people of Zion from the evils that are manifest among us; evils of irreligion, intemperance, lightmindedness and folly of every description.

With this great obligation in view, it stands to reason that our labors should consist of something more than simply supplying an entertainment, for the people to be amused at for an hour or two in the week. The exercises upon which reports are required by the General Superintendency of the Y. M. M. I. A., are of such a nature that if persistently engaged in, cannot fail to awaken an interest in the real studies of life. They are expressly designed to cultivate a taste for Scriptural and doctrinal investigations, and to direct the minds of the young men of Zion in channels of research, that will lead them to treasures of miscellaneous knowledge. A glance at the new Roll and Record Book which has lately been prepared for the Associations shows that, if the exercises are rendered and the record is kept, future reports will exhibit the attendance at the meetings, the number of subjective lectures delivered under the following headings: Bible, Book of Mormon, Doctrine and Covenants, Doctrinal, Church History, Historical, Scientific, Biographical, Political, Travel, Miscellaneous, and the number of Testimonies borne, Essays read, Declamations rendered, Musical exercises, Missionary appointments filled and Questions answered.

Let these exercises be found in every Association, in the varied forms in which they will naturally be delivered, and, if continued any length of time, they will show substantial progress in thought and wonderful improvement in the religious sentiment of our young people.

But it is outside of the meetings of the Associations where much good can be done, and where systematic work should be performed by officers and members. It is our duty by example and precept to save the erring; to turn the footsteps of those who are going astray into paths of virtue, temperance, honesty and gentleness; that there may be an end put to the damning sins of licentiousness, that occasionally crop out among our young people, and to drunkenness, dishonesty, and hoodlumism; all of which are reproaches upon us and are entirely foreign to the spirit and intent of the work in which we are engaged. Let us systematize our efforts to correct these evils and never rest until we succeed in rooting them out. The labor we perform on the outside in these directions will do more to fill up our meeting houses, and make the prescribed order of exercises interesting than any amount of ingenuity displayed by the programme committees, in their endeavors to please the fancy of the large congregations drawn together for the purpose of being amused.

ZION'S CHORAL UNION has been organized under the most favorable auspices, with bright promises for its future success, the first meeting being held in the City Hall, November 22nd. The combination of talent in its leading spirits insures an organization that will be a pride to our music loving people. Prof. George Careless is the conductor, and Profs. E. Beesley and Evan Stephens assistants. The famous cantata, "Belshazzar," has been selected for the initial exercise. We wish the Choral Union lasting prosperity and a reign of perfect harmony.

———

In the September number of THE CONTRIBUTOR, Vol. VII., page 465, the writer upon "The Great Pyramid," falls into an error, using the following words: "I have been told that Apostle Orson Pratt, substituting the present English for the cubit inch, found that the step occurs at the inch marking one thousand eight hundred and thirty," etc. The reverse is true; Apostle Pratt, adhering to the Egyptian cubit, pursued his calculations so carefully, as to discover that the Pyramid measurement, indicated not only the year 1830, but the day and hour when the Church was organized at Fayette, New York.

———

A very gratifying indication that the spirit of improvement is increasing among is, is found in the organization of libraries and free reading rooms. There has been a very large increase in the number of books in the Association libraries during the past year, and free reading rooms have been opened for the winter at Logan, Provo, Manti, Spanish Fork and a number of other settlements. In nearly ever town in the Territory these reading rooms might be established, and if properly conducted, would do a great deal of good. It is à credit to any town to have a pleasantly lighted and warmed room, where the people may assemble and read the current literature of the day, and study over the writings of the wise and learned of all ages. The Y. M. M. I. A., should take the lead in such enterprises and establish suitable rules for the maintenance of good order. We would suggest that a record of the number of volumes supplied to readers should be strictly kept. Such a record will be of great interest hereafter as indicating the relative increase of interest in the reading habit from year to year. The publishers of THE CONTRIBUTOR will take pleasure in sending a copy of the magazine *gratis* to all of the free reading rooms opened and conducted under the auspices of the Associations.

———

SKETCHES AND REMINISCENCES OF PRISON LIFE.

I.

HAVING been convicted in the court of the Third Judicial District of Utah, of unlawful cohabitation, and not being a "promising young man," I was sentenced one fine day in the autumn of 1885, to imprisonment in the Utah Penitentiary for six months, and to pay a fine of three hundred dollars and costs, the monetary part of the payment amounting in all to four hundred and twenty-five dollars. To this liberal dose of alleged justice—at that time, according to the "construction of the courts," the full penalty of the law—his honor Chief Justice Zane threw in, as an unsolicited gratuity, a severe lecture, the strictures of which were hurled at the writer and his religion, winding up with the comforting assurance that both would yet be "ground to powder" under the wheel of the legal Juggernaut car, of which, for the time being, he appeared to be acting as teamster.

Before going to my winter residence, of which I was soon to become an inmate from necessity, I was permitted, in company of an officer, to call upon and bid adieu to those loved better than life. The parting was exceedingly painful on both sides, and it were better that upon that picture the veil of forgetfulness be dropped.

Before leaving the city I called upon my friend A. H. Cannon, who was very ill from a protracted attack of typhoid fever. Much as I desired to see him I regretted my visit, on account of the pain it caused him. The effect produced upon him made it necessary for me to struggle hard to suppress my own emotions. Being weak from the effects of disease he did not possess that control over his feelings that he would have exercised had he been stronger. Taking my hand in his own, his great heart swelled with sympathetic kindness and, while the tears rolled down his cheeks, he murmured in broken accents; "I wish I could go in your stead."

I had two companions in durance vile: Andrew Smith and Emil Olsen. Accompanied by a number of friends, we arrived at the prison about three o'clock in the afternoon. After taking our heights and weights and whatever valuables, in the shape of penknives and odd change, we had, we were ushered by the turnkey through the ponderous gate into the enclosure, which is nearly an acre in extent, the boundary being a thick wall, twenty feet high.

Andrew Smith and myself entered simultaneously. The greeting with which we were saluted was more than sufficiently demonstrative, yet to me it was strickingly unsatisfactory. This estimate was based on the fact that it was neither amiable nor complimentary. A crowd of convicts were congregated in the long, low wooden building where Uncle Sam's semi-cooked provisions were at feeding hours, discussed by his guests. As soon as the word passed around that "fresh fish"—as new arrivals are designated—had been delivered, there was a general scramble to get a sight of us. Then went up a terrific shout, which rent the air, so to speak, and sent a cold chill down my spinal column; not that I was afflicted with any sensation of timidity, but rather because my estimate of the quality of the company I would have to keep for half a year had received such a precipitate confirmation. Some of the gentler and more refined of the exclamations of our newly found friends were: "Kill him, d—n him! Hang him! Lynch him!"

Of course it quickly dawned upon me that those forcible but inelegant expressions of feeling were directed toward my companion, who in his capacity of policeman, had not gained the unmitigated affection of the criminal class. Andrew seemed to take it as a matter of course, and we were soon surrounded by a number of friends, who had landed in the institution by the same path which had taken us to it. From them we received a loving greeting, although its expression was liable to be taken, except in the spirit of it, either of two ways. "We are sorry to see you here," they exclaimed. But we were there, and if they had not been in a position to see us they would have been somewhere else, which would have suited them precisely. It would also have suited us, for their sakes. So also would it have suited them for us not to be there, for our sakes.

Shortly after my instalment as a guest of the government I was called to the gate by direction of the Warden, in order that I might be completely initiated as a full fledged graduate. Mr. Curtis conducted me to the butcher shop, where he placed me in the hands of the barber. As I seated myself in a huge chair, which was singularly devoid of ornamentation, the Knight of the Scissors said:

"Shall I cut his hair?"

The turnkey took a birdseye view of my cranium, and seeing that the hirsute growth thereon was the reverse of abundant, he said:

"No. Take off his beard."

This facial adornment was one of the most luxuriant in Utah. The young man tied a string around it as near to the roots as practicable and slashed into it with a huge pair of scissors. At my request he wrapped it in a piece of paper that it might be preserved. Having been deprived of the privilege of wearing it on the place designed by nature, I have ever since worn it in my trunk.

Not having previously shaved clean for over twenty years, the scraping process was not pleasant. However it was a slight improvement on grubbing sagebrush, and I uttered no complaint. If I had, it would have made no difference, as I was fully impressed with the consideration that that razor was being propelled by the entire population of the United States, so to speak, numbering "fifty-five millions," more or less.

Some strange coincidents occur in a man's life. In conversation with the barber I discovered his identity. We will call him John Ricards, for convenience' sake. About twenty years before my shaving experience, while I was a missionary in Great Britain, I visited the house of his parents. He was at that time a small baby, and I have some recollection of taking him in my arms, being naturally fond of children. The next time I met him was in the above described capacity.   •

As I passed out of the barber—butcher-shop into the outer court-yard I beheld Andrew Smith, seated on a bench. He had already undergone the barbarous process. His auburn beard was no more, and I was struck with the wealth of space his countenance exhibited when fully exposed to view. When he saw me, he seemed a little startled, and then broke into a laugh at my expense. His hilarity was pardonable.

I was taken into the Warden's office, a very small apartment in which the convicts' clothing was stored and where Mr. Dow also conducted the manufacture of young chickens by means of an incubator. I may here interpolate that he was quite successful in running this miniature chicken factory. There I was uniformed in government clothing, conspicuous for its encircling stripes of black and grey, causing the wearer to appear like one of the zebras of John Robinson's menagerie. After donning my new pantaloons, like every other man under similar circumstances, I made a dive with both hands for the pockets. One landed all right, but the other slid down my leg on the outside.

"There is only one pocket," said Mr. Curtis.

"That reminds me," said I, "of the process that brought me here."

"How is that?"

"Exceedingly one-sided."

When I re-entered the prison proper I stood by the corner of one of the build-ings, while I was greeted with audible smiles from some of the brethren. Others expressed some degree of wrath in my behalf, but I felt very much like a sheep who had been shorn and left to shiver in the cold, and it is to be presumed that my expression bore some resemblance to that meek and gentle quadruped. It would not, however, have taken much to have made as radical a change in my feelings as had been made in my appearance. A trifling incitement would have created an active desire to kick somebody. If that revolution of sentiment had taken place, and an opportunity been afforded to hit the proper spot, it is doubtful if even the oft-quoted fifty-five millions would have prevented its vigorous administration.

At the time I became an inmate of the prison what is known as the dining hall, where the convicts take their meals, was a dingy and comfortless apartment. It is much more cheerful and more appropriately appointed now than then. Large skylights have been added, giving additional light, which was greatly needed. The room is fifty-four feet long by nineteen wide. The material used in its construction is simply inch weather boarding, nailed to a studding frame, the timbers being set at unusually wide distances apart. The height to the square is about seven feet six inches. There is no ceiling, the bare shingles being the only obstacle between the inmates and the heavenly expanse. The cross braces by which the frame of the roof is stayed are generally adorned with shirts, stockings, and articles of underwear generally, making the place smack somewhat of "Rag Fair," London. Occasionally from the same raised position a couple of "exalted soles"—hob-nailed attachments to a dilapidated pair of boots—look grimly down from where they are suspended.

No part of the interior is plastered, there being but an inch board to the weather. Here and there the thin walls are plastered over with gaudy pictures clipped from periodicals of the day, according to the taste or fancy of the convict whose seat happens to be near the particular spot thus decorated. For convenience' sake, little narrow shelves have been nailed to the wall, and on these are old fruit cans, the tin pint cup with which each convict is furnished, and other articles.

Against the wall, and skirting the entire room, at the height of an ordinary table, is a rough deal board, two feet wide. This serves for a table. Each convict fortunate enough to secure a place at this board is allotted a space of twenty-two inches in width, giving barely enough elbow room at meal times. The seating convenience at this table consists of a rough plank, two inches thick and eight inches wide, supported, a short distance outward from the side-table, upon uprights consisting of pieces of the same material. The seating space allotted to each is of the same length as and parallel with the tabular apportionment.

As over one hundred men sit down at each meal, the room is, as may well be imagined, at such times always crowded. Consequently the side-tables are far from being sufficient, and there are four or five large tables besides, ranged down the centre of the room. But they are not so popular with the convicts as the seats along the wall, owing to the latter perhaps being slightly more retired, if such a term could be appropriately used in connection with so great a crowd. At the table to which I was assigned, I had the pleasure of being sandwiched between George Romney and Andrew Smith. W. A. Rossiter and Edward Brain were also adjacent. At the evening meal of the first day the bench upon which the last named gentleman was seated gave away and he suddenly and involuntarily assumed a horizontal position, causing the solemn remark: "Behold the Brain of the penitentiary spread out on the floor." He was gathered up and demurely discussed his allowance of bread and sugarless tea in an attitude similiar to that maintained by the naughty boy of the story, who had undergone the operation known as "spanking."

The bill of fare was not ravishingly sumptuous. The morning meal consisted of two pieces of bread, a piece of meat dumped upon a tin plate, a couple of potatoes, and a tin pint cupful of alleged coffee, minus sugar and milk. The potatoes were not of the "mammoth" variety, but might properly have been classed as infinitessimals, with occasional exceptions. Like most of those whose duty it was to devour them, they were invariably "sad." This tendency to melancholy was superinduced by the fact that they were, owing to the smallness of the kitchen range, cooked the night previous. As a consequence they were generally about as mealy as a bar of Snell's Pale Sapone soap.

On alternate days the meat and pensive potatoes were substituted by a mysterious compound called hash. Not having any means of analysis I am unable to state its constituents. Owing to its inexplicability I generally gave it a wide berth. There was one man among the prisoners, however, who had acquired a deep affection for this particular dish. He was a young fellow with a large cavernous mouth, a face beaming with pimples in place of intelligence, and whose pantaloons were always tattered about the feet. Besides he always wore them so low down at the seat that it seemed as if it might act as a kind of hobble, to prevent him from taking strides of sufficient length to enable him to make a successful escape, had he attempted such a thing. Added to these characteristics he had a piping voice, whose mellifluous tones were heard every hash morning, singing: "Who's got any hash they don't want?" He collected great quantities, with which he would stuff himself until he became a sort of animated sausage.

I gazed upon this young man and wondered whether there might possibly be any other position in life for which he was adapted, besides those of convict and hash consumer, when I was struck with a brilliant idea. What a bonanza he would be to that class of sectarian Gospel-dispensers who, after a brief sojourn in Utah, transform themselves into hairbreadth escape heroes, betake themselves to the East, where they graphically depict their valorous deeds, the fearful and dangerous condition of Mormon society, in the midst of which they had to mount the pulpit with a Colt's revolver in one hand and the Bible in the other. When the soft spots in the heads, hearts and pockets of the Eastern gullibles are touched the services of the youth in question could be utilized to advantage. As a plate-passer he has few equals, and probably no superiors. Should he prove as great a success as a collector of dimes as he showed himself to be as a gatherer of hash he would doubtless prove a valuable acquisition to the average anti-Mormon professional falsifier for pelf. Why should genius in such a useful direction be compelled

"To bloom unseen,
And waste its sweetness on the desert air."

of the penitentiary?

Meat and bread with the potato accompaniment composed the midday meal one day and the next—alternating regularly—it consisted simply of soup and bread. As a general thing the soup was not of a nature to entitle it to the designation of "liquid nourishment." While its liquidity could not be questioned, nutrimentality was not a conspicuous factor of its composition. Its attractiveness was not increased by its lukewarm condition. It reminded me of a story I had read of a poverty-stricken old Englishman who applied to a parson for relief. "My friend," said the dispenser of theoretical religion, "the Scriptures say that man shall not live by bread alone." "Well, yes," replied the hungry man, "I believe it is better to have a few wegetables with it." I always thought that "a few wegetables" would have been a desirable addition to the soup. The caterers for the convicts appeared, however, to consider them a superfluity. Soup dinners were not in high favor as they were productive of a subsequent goneness, but the evening meal, which was without a shadow of turning, was the most attenuated. Its sole constituents were a couple of pieces of dry bread and a pint cupful of tea—always without milk or sugar.

For a while after I entered the Utah bastile the only knife and fork we had at meal times was an iron spoon, which is not an implement specially adapted for carving' or impaling provender. As a consequence we had to resort to a liberal use of the fingers, after the manner of the untutored savage who roams over the arid plains of the great Northwest. During one of my first experiences in that line, I was laboring assiduously on a chunk of beef, which I held in one hand while a soggy potato reposed in the other. Friend Romney was similarly engrossed. Turning to me he remarked, with much gravity: "If our families were to see us in this fix, there would not be a dry eye in the audience." Involuntarily his own eyes suffused with the indications of emotion, while I began to feel as if half of the unconsumed potato had stuck somewhere in my throat, and a couple of liquid beads ran down my nose and were absorbed by Uncle Sam's victuals on the plate in front of me. The average Mormon cohabitation convict may not give much heed to his own condition, but allusions to his loved ones strike him in a tender spot.

The reason why the use of knives and forks had been temporarily suspended was a substantial one. Some of the prisoners were not fastidious in regard to the manner in which they employed these articles. Some who had a predilection for the severe styles of practical joking occasionally stuck them into a fellow convict, as had been the case with Mike Sullivan, who jabbed a fork into one man's back, coming pretty near making a corpse of him. Another desperate young man had made a lunge with a similar implement at the throat of Mr. Curtis, the turnkey, and came very near perforating that gentleman's jugular. It was therefore a matter for congratulation rather than grief, that those mischievous articles, in the hands of dangerous men, were dispensed with. After a while, however, a number of us were allowed to obtain pocket knives, with which we managed to get along with comparative comfort.

O. W. W. T.

ASSOCIATION INTELLIGENCE.

THE new Roll and Record Book is ready for distribution and may be procured on application to the General Secretary, Nephi W. Clayton, or at THE CONTRIBUTOR Office. The book holds twelve hundred names and is made of the best paper, finely ruled and printed. The price is seventy-five cents, on receipt of which, it will be sent by mail to any address. Every Association should at once be supplied with this book, that the records of all may be uniform.

AN interesting exercise is being introduced in some of the Associations in Salt Lake City. It is the reading of the "news of the week" by one of the members, who is required to jot down items of interest that occur during the week and to read the budget thus prepared at the meeting. Where care is shown in the selection of news, this exercise is not only interesting but quite instructive. Items pertaining to the work of the Associations should form a conspicuous part of these news budgets.

THE Conference of the Y. M. M. I. A. of the Weber Stake of Zion was held on Sunday, November 7, 1886, in the Ogden Tabernacle. There were present, Presidents L. W. Shurtliff and C. F. Middleton, Elders West, Badger and Burton, of the General Superintendency, and the members of the Central Board, also presidents from nearly all the Associations in the county. The house was comfortably filled with listeners. The congregation was called to order by Elder Z. Ballantyne. After the opening exercises, the arranged programme was presented: An address on "Christ's visit to the Nephites on this continent," was given by Elder George H. Carver, of Plain City; followed by an able essay on "Prayer and Fasting," written by William Purdy, and read by George Browning, of the Second Ward, Ogden. An unusually interesting dissertation on the "First Four Principles of the Gospel" was listened to from Elder Josiah L.

Ferrin, of Eden, which was followed by a lively and instructive address by W. H. Crandall, of Pleasant View, in which he explained his "Reasons for being a Mormon." Elder Moroni Poulter, of the Fourth Ward, related some "Anecdotes of Men's Integrity to Principle;" which closed the exercises of the forenoon.

At two p. m., the tabernacle was well filled. After the opening song and prayer, the sacrament of the Lord's supper was administered. Secretary Angus T. Wright, then presented the general and local authorities of the Y. M. M. I. A., all of which were unanimously sustained. Elder H. H. Thomas, of the Third Ward Association, gave a biographical sketch of George Stevenson. The numerous interesting incidents in the experience of this celebrated inventor who first applied steam as a motive power, were ably recited to the audience, and the various traits of the man's character were carefully pointed out.

Secretary A. T. Wright read reports from a number of the Associations setting forth briefly their condition and labors. The audience was then favored with able and practical addresses from Elders Rodney Badger, W. S. Burton and Joseph A. West, whose instructions were listened to with marked attention.

The following brethren were called to act as missionaries during the ensuing six months: P. C. Stephenson, West Harrisville; Reuben Reese, Pleasant View; George Butler, Marriotts; L. C. Carter, Lynne; C. A. Smurthwaite, Third Ward, Ogden; Washington Jenkins, Second Ward Ogden; Josiah L. Ferrin, Eden; Henry Child, Riverdale.

The conference adjourned for six months. A meeting of the officers was held during the noon hour, in which practical instruction was given concerning the Associations by Superintendents E. H. Anderson, Joseph A. West and Elder Z. Ballantyne. The associations in this Stake are steadly gaining in attraction and usefulness.

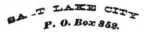

THE CONTRIBUTOR.

VOLUME EIGHT. 1886-7.

THE CONTRIBUTOR COMPANY takes pleasure in announcing the commencement of a new volume of The Contributor with the NOVEMBER* number.

The progress of the Magazine, in developing home literature, promoting the growth of Mutual Improvement Associations, which it represents, and cultivating a superior taste for reading matter among the people, is well known. It stands in these respects at the head of all our local publications. It contains more original matter, in better shape for preservation than any magazine published in the interest of our people. Following are some of the leading features that will distinguish

VOLUME EIGHT.

The Rise and Fall of Nauvoo, By Elder B. H. Roberts, Leading Church History Series. Illustrated with fine, full page engravings—each a Souvenir of Nauvoo—embracing the following views: The Mansion, Nauvoo House, Old Parade Ground, Temple in Ruins, Joseph's Store House, Corner Stone of Nauvoo House (in which Original Manuscript of Book of Mormon was found), Residences of Brigham Young, Heber C. Kimball, Wilford Woodruff, Edward Hunter, Daniel H. Wells, and others, and PORTRAIT OF SIDNEY RIGDON.

Notable Indians of Mexico, By Apostle Moses Thatcher. An account of some of the leading men of Mexico, from personal observations, and including descriptions of Mexican scenes

The Religions of Christendom, A series of articles explanatory of the faith and church observances of the principal religious denominations, by their leading ministers in Utah. The first of these, "The Episcopal Faith," by Rev. G. D. B. Miller, will appear in the November number.

Why I am a Mormon, By several of our best writers, explanatory of the faith of the Latter-day Saints, and experiences leading to its adoption by the writers.

The North Countries, A description of Scandinavian lands and people, including an account of the "Land of the Midnight Sun."

Biblical Cosmogony, By Thos. W. Brookbank. A scientific treatise upon the formation and development of the earth, harmonizing the Scriptural and natural evidences of the creation.

The Eastern Question. A series of eight papers upon this interesting topic which has for so many years been the subject of dispute and warfare between the Great Powers of Europe. The articles are from the talented pen of Elder J. M. Tanner, now in Constantinople, and his personal observations of countries and people, will add a peculiar interest to the series.

Christmas Story, A Prize of Twenty-five Dollars and THE CONTRIBUTOR SOUVENIR MEDAL will be given for the best Christmas Story. Short Stories will also appear periodically in the volume.

The Prize Christmas Poem, And the best poetical contributions of our local poets will adorn the volume.

Comments of the Day, Will take up the existing situation of the Latter-day Saints, religious, political and social, expressing the views thereon of some of our leading authorities. It will be contributed to by President Joseph F. Smith, Apostles Moses Thatcher, F. M. Lyman, John Henry Smith, and several others, "whose voices speak with no uncertain sound."

The Editorial and Association Intelligence Departments will be replete with instructive information relating to the Associations and the general interests of our young people. Officers of the Associations are requested to contribute freely to these departments.

We thank the public for past patronage, and ask its continuation for the future. Subscription: $2.00 a year, in advance. SUBSCRIBERS PAYING $2.25, IN ADVANCE, are entitled to have the volume BOUND at the end of the year, FREE, Send in your subscriptions without delay.

ADDRESS:

THE CONTRIBUTOR CO.,
40 Main Street, SALT LAKE CITY.

Remittances should be made by P. O. note, money order, registered letter or draft.

* In consequence of a disappointment in the type procured for the New Volume; we were compelled to order a new fount by telegraph. The delay thus caused, and other reasons which we think will promote the welfare of the magazine have determined us to begin the volume with the NOVEMBER Number, instead of the October Number as heretofore.

Lightning Source UK Ltd.
Milton Keynes UK
UKHW020316111218
333787UK00006B/189/P

9 780483 776104